TROLLEYBUSES
IN PORTUGAL

DAVID HARVEY

AMBERLEY

Front cover: UTIC-bodied 6, which opened the Oporto system. It is in its very smart red and white livery and grey roof, but has already had its windscreen modified by being fitted with a glazed opening windscreen. The trolleybus has crossed the top level of the Ponte de Dom Luis I bridge and is working through Vila Nova de Gaia on the 33 route to Coimbões. It is being overtaken by an Austin Mini at a time when British-built cars were still being exported to Portugal. (D. R. Harvey Collection)

Rear cover: The crew of trolleybus 6 take their break in the shadows cast by one of the buildings at the Gualtar terminus. This was at the eastern end of the 5 route. The layout of these two-door Drögmöller-bodied Henschel O Bus II 6500 trolleybuses, with only centre and rear doors, made them unsuitable for one-man operation, hence the use of a conductor. (D. R. Harvey Collection)

First published 2019

Amberley Publishing
The Hill, Stroud
Gloucestershire, GL5 4EP

www.amberley-books.com

British Library Cataloguing in Publication Data.
A catalogue record for this book is available from the British Library.

ISBN 978 1 4456 9283 8 (print)
ISBN 978 1 4456 9284 5 (ebook)

Typeset in 10pt on 13pt Sabon.
Typesetting by Aura Technology and Software Services, India.
Printed in the UK.

Contents

Introduction

There were just three trolleybus systems in Portugal. These consisted of one small and short-lived system, (Braga) one medium sized fleet that is still operating but at a much reduced size, (Coimbra) and one large system with a fleet totalling some 126 vehicles of which 50 were double-deckers (Oporto). In all cases the trolleybuses were intended to replace the existing tram fleet, but only in Braga did this actually happen. In Coimbra, many of the twenty strong tram fleet were retained in the transport museum while the trolleybus system declined. The system limped on from the early 1990s, surviving into 2019 but as a shadow of its former self. The large Oporto trolleybus thrived from when it opened in 1959 until 1993, when the services across the River Douro were abandoned in July of that year. The two isolated routes to Ermesinde and Travagem were converted to motorbuses in early 1994, as were the double-deck services to the east of the city, which were abruptly ended in March 1994. This was due to the building of a road viaduct at Areosa, which cut the trolleybuses off from their depot. The remaining 49 trolleybuses were put into store until 25 of them were returned to service in late 1996. This was to be but a small interregnum on the three routes as the system finally closed on 27 December 1997.

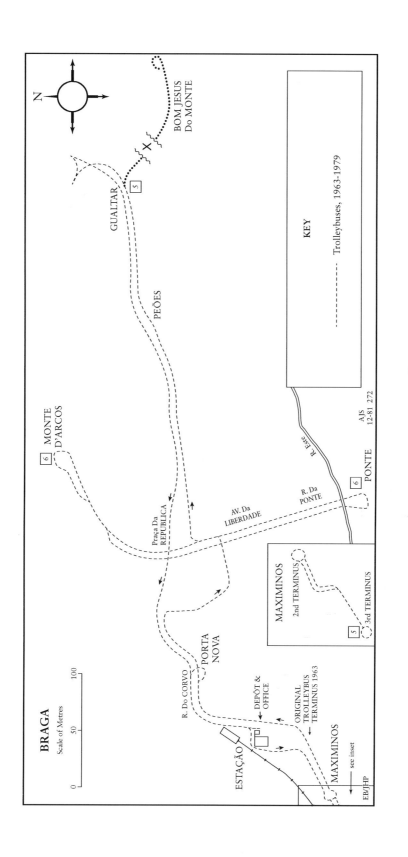

BRAGA

Scale of Metres

0   50   100

N

ESTAÇÃO

R. Do CORVO

PORTA NOVA

DEPOT & OFFICE

ORIGINAL TROLLEYBUS TERMINUS 1963

MAXIMINOS

see inset

EB/JHP

MONTE D'ARCOS   6

Praça Da REPUBLICA

AV. Da LIBERDADE

R. Da PONTE

PONTE   6

R. Este

PEÕES

GUALTAR

5

BOM JESUS Do MONTE

MAXIMINOS

2nd TERMINUS

3rd TERMINUS   5

KEY

-------- Trolleybuses, 1963-1979

AJS
12-81 272

Braga

Braga began trolleybus operations in quite unusual circumstances. On 30 December 1960, the German city of Heilbronn in northern Baden-Württemberg closed down its complete two-route trolleybus system that had only opened on 23 September 1951. Nine of the twelve-strong fleet of trolleybuses were bought by Braga to replace the tram system whose infrastructure was in poor condition, especially in regard to the extremely worn tram tracks. The trolleybus fleet consisted of three MANs with Kässbohrer three door bodies, numbered 1–3, dating from 1960, and six older 1951-vintage Henschels with locally-built Drogmöller bodywork, numbered 4–9. Additionally the overhead wiring, traction poles, rectifiers, switch gear and spares were also purchased.

The nine trolleybuses were ready for operation when the system opened on 28 May 1963 but despite the time lag of two years, they all eventually entered service in the Heilbronn livery of cream with a blue waistband and were numbered 1–9. They were repainted during 1967 in the SOTUBE livery of cherry red and cream with a grey roof. There were only ever two trolleybus routes forming a cross shape with the Praça da Republica at the hub of the two services; the 5 went from Gualtar via the railway station to Maximinos near to the Bom Jesus funicular, while the 6 route went from Ponte just over the bridge over the River Este to Monte d'Arios. This route was abandoned in 1973 but the 5 route survived until the end of 1979. Two of the Henschels, 7 and 8 were rebodied by CAMO as late as 1975 and were sold to Coimbra as their 48 and 49, though it is doubtful if they were ever operated. The Braga trolleybus system was rather camera shy and many of the vehicles had indistinct or no fleet numbers.

Braga Trolleybus Fleet

FLEET NO	REG NO	CHASSIS	NO	ELECTRIC EQUIP	BODY	SEATS	NEW/ ACQU	OUT	NOTES
1	-	MAM MKE2	100627/1	Siemens-Schuckert	Kässbohrer	B29T	1960 2/1967	1980	Ex-Heilbronn 207
2	-	"	100627/3	"	"	B29T	1960 2/1967	1980	Ex-Heilbronn 208
3	-	"	100660/42	"	"	B29T	1960 2/1967	1980	Ex-Heilbronn 209
4	-	Henschel O Bus II 6500	25233		Drögmöller	B23D	1951 2/1967	10/1976	Ex-Heilbronn 201

5	-	"	25235		"	B23D	1951 2/1967	10/1976	Ex-Heilbronn 202
6	-	"	25230		"	B23D	1951 2/1967	10/1976	Ex-Heilbronn 203
7	-	"	25231		"	B23D	1951 2/1967	1980	Ex-Heilbronn 204 Reb. CAMO B36D 1975. To Coimbra 48, 1980
8	-	"	25234		"	B23D	1951 2/1967	1980	Ex-Heilbronn 205 Reb. CAMO B36D 1975. To Coimbra 49, 1980
9	-	"	25232		"	B23D	1951 2/1967	5/1972	Ex-Heilbronn 206

Formerly 207 in the abandoned Heilbronn system, MAN MKE2 trolleybus 1 is in red, white and grey livery after the SOTUBE takeover in February 1967. It stands before pulling away when barely a quarter full. The Kässbohrer three door bodywork had ten small windows on the offside, which gave the vehicles an almost Italian-appearance. Carrying an advertisement for Mabor tyres on the rather neat trolley shroud on the roof, a noticeable feature of these vehicles were the artillery-style front wheels. (SOTUBE)

Above: The three door layout of trolleybus 2 shows the high floor line of these trolleybuses. Although built in 1960 for the German Heilbronn system in northern Baden-Württemberg as that fleet's 208, the design of the Kässbohrer B29T bodywork looked as if it was an earlier 1950s product. The trolleybus has lost its trolley shrouds and is painted in the attractive SOTUBE livery of red-painted lower panels, white window surrounds and a light grey roof. (D. R. Harvey Collection)

Below: On 28 July 1967, still in the Heilbronn livery of cream with a blue waistband, MAN MKE2 trolleybus 3 carries the ubiquitous advertisement for Mabor tyres on the trolley shrouds above the centre doors. The steep steps into the saloon must have been something of a hazard for the young, elderly and infirm. A feature of these Kässbohrer was the stylized ventilation slots behind the rear door and the large numbered saloon windows. (R. Symons)

Above: MAN MKE2 with a Kässbohrer B29T body is parked in the turning circle at the Maximinos terminus just beyond the trolleybus depot. The Germanic-styled bodywork looks slightly out of place in the heat of the Portuguese summer. The three newest trolleybuses were numbered 1–3 in the Braga fleet and looked much older than their seven years when brought into use in the Portuguese city. (D. R. Harvey Collection)

Below: The older batch of Henschel trolleybuses had Drögmöller bodies with centre and rear doors, a seating capacity of only twenty-three and an undisclosed number of standee passengers. This trolleybus is still in its original Heilbronn livery and stands in the Praça da Republica. Soon after it was sold to Braga as their fleet number 5. It is working on a short route to Porto on the western half of the 5 route. (D. R. Harvey Collection)

Above: The crew of trolleybus 6 take their break in the shadows cast by one of the buildings at the Gualtar terminus. This was at the eastern end of the 5 route. The layout of these two door Drögmöller-bodied Henschel O Bus II 6500 trolleybuses, with only centre and rear doors, made them unsuitable for one-man operation, hence the use of a conductor. (D. R. Harvey Collection)

Below: Henschel O Bus II 6500 trolleybus 6, built in 1951, stands in the centre of Braga with its Drögmöller B23D bodywork positively gleaming in the SOTUBE livery of cherry red and cream with a grey roof. Acquired from Heilbronn in February 1967, their wide pair of doors made for fairly easy loading and unloading (although a notice in Portuguese stating 'Cuidado com os degraus', or 'mind the steps', might have been useful) but these centre/rear doored trolleybuses were certainly not suitable for o-m-o work. (D. R. Harvey Collection)

Above: At Peões about halfway along the eastern section of the 5 route to Gualtar on 29 July 1967, barely three weeks after the SOTUBE takeover, is Henschel O Bus II 6500 trolleybus 7. This Drögmöller B23T trolleybus was formerly Heibronn 201 and was new in 1951. In many ways the design of the body made them look modern when compared to the three younger MAN trolleybuses. (R. Symons)

Below: Rebodied Henschel O Bus II 6500 trolleybus 7 is travelling away from the Praça da Republica over the cobbled road surface when heading westwards on the 5 trolleybus service to Maximinos on 26 July 1977. It would be fair to acknowledge that this twenty-six year old chassis belies its years due to the modern 1975-built CAMO two door thirty-six seater body. The deep windscreen and the large saloon windows are typical of the bodies being built for bus chassis in Portugal at this time. (D. R. Harvey Collection)

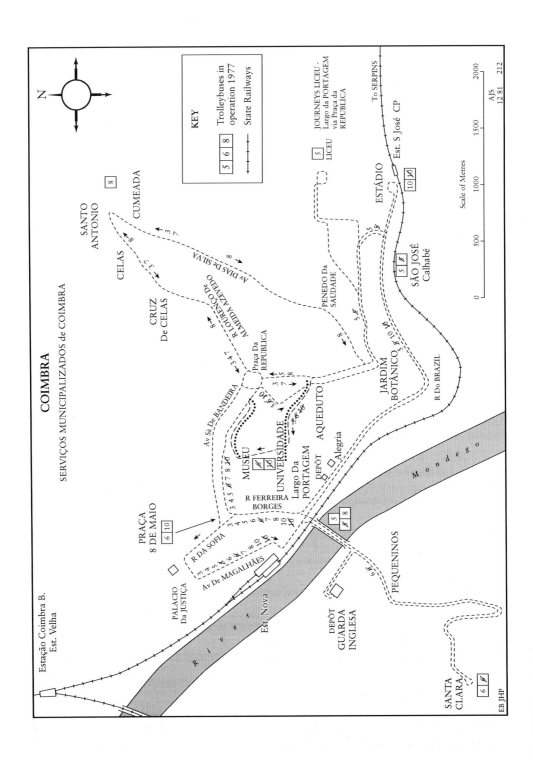

SMTUC, Coimbra

Coimbra stands on the east bank of the River Montego and consists of a picturesque lower shopping centre near to the river with narrow side streets and alleyways leading off the Rua Ferreira Borges, an area devoted to the ancient university town, while the higher areas are mainly residential.

A metre gauge electric tram system was introduced in 1910 by the SMTUC (Servigos Municipalizados de Transportes Urbanos de Coimbra) and by 1940, the tram fleet numbered some twenty cars.

In February 1947, after the opening of the new Santa Clara Bridge over the River Montego, Coimbra began operating the first trolleybuses in Portugal on the 6 route over the bridge to the model village of Pequeninos and then to the Santa Clara monastery. This experimental route used just a pair of Swiss-built Saurer STP with Saurer B22D bodywork numbered 21 and 22 directly following on from the last tram in the fleet.

In 1951, six Park Royal bodied Sunbeam MF2Bs numbered 23–28 were bought in order to take over the Sao José tram route 5. These had very British-looking bodies, resembling somewhat the small mid-1930s single-decker trolleybuses built for Wolverhampton Corporation. In 1954, three more Park Royal bodied trolleybuses entered service, though this time with BUT LETB1 chassis' built by Leyland, which became numbers 29–31 in the Coimbra trolleybus fleet. Trolleybuses 22–28 were rebodied by Salvador Caetano in 1974 and in 1979 the BUTs were similarly rebodied. Finally, Saurer 21 was rebodied by UTIC in 1979. UTIC's Lisbon factory bodied ten new BUT LETB1s in 1958, which were numbered 32–41. Finally, six Sunbeam MF2Bs numbered 42–47 were delivered in 1962, again with UTIC bodywork.

In 1980, two CAMO rebodied Henschel trolleybuses (originally new in 1951) working in Heibronn, West Germany, were bought from Braga for spares, the system having closed in 1979.

Twenty new trolleybuses were bought in 1983 and were numbered 50-69. These were Caetano/EFACEC 190TR110s, with rather 'boxy'-looking Salvador Caetano bodies. A solitary articulated trolleybus was purchased from Oporto in September 2003 where it had been numbered 167. A single Caetano/EFACEC 175TR110, formerly STCP 74 was acquired in September 2003 and was given the fleet number 71.

Until 1972 there were two depots used by trolleybuses, the original tram depot in the Rua de Alegria and a second one in Rua de Sofia. A new riverside bus and trolleybus depot at the Guarda Inglesa was opened in 1972 with the tram fleet returning to the Rua de Alegria until the shutdown of the system on 14 February 1980.

This trolleybus system had a love-hate relationship to its trolleybus services, which used mainly British built trolleybus chassis. It gradually replaced Coimbra's tramway network, which closed in January 1980 and, like the trams, had a long period of slow decline. The British trolleybuses were all withdrawn by 1993 when the system seemed doomed. By 2000, with most of trolleybuses withdrawn, there was a change in policy and ten of the 1983 batch of Caetano/EFACEC 190TR110s were refurbished for further service. The Coimbra trolleybus fleet now comprises of just twelve vehicles.

Coimbra Trolleybus Fleet

FLEET NO	REG NO	CHASSIS	NO	ELECTRIC EQUIP	BODY	SEATS	NEW/ ACQU	OUT	NOTES
21		Saurer 3TP		Secheron	Saurer	B22D	1947	1984	Reb. UTIC B24D 1979
22		"			"	"	"	1987	Reb. S.Caetano B28D 1974
23		Sunbeam MF2B	80065	BTH 125 hp	Park Royal	B40D	1950	6/1993	1950 CMS Earls Court exhibit. Reb. S.Caetano B33D 1974
24		"	80066	"	"	"	"	by 1993	Reb. S.Caetano B33D 1979
25		"	80061	"	"	"	"		Reb. S.Caetano B34D 1974
26		"	80064	"	"	"	"		Reb. S.Caetano B34D 1979
27		"	80063	"	"	"	"		Reb. S.Caetano B34D 1974
28		"	80062	"	"	"	"		Reb. S.Caetano B34D 1974
29		Leyland LETB1	540133	BTH	Park Royal	B32D	1954		Reb. S.Caetano B32D 1979
30		"	540132	"	"	B32D	1954		Reb. S.Caetano B32D 1979

31		"	532622	"	"	B32D	1954	by1993	
32		Leyland /BUT LETB1	573042	"	"	B32D	1957		
33		"	573044	"	"	B32D	1957		
34		"	573145	"	"	B32D	1957		
35		"	573043	"	"	B32D	1957		
36		Leyland /BUT LETB1	610081	AEI	UTIC	B32D	1961		
37		"	610154	"	"	B32D	1961		
38		"	610133	"	"	B32D	1961		
39		"	610168	"	"	B32D	1961		
40		"	610148	"	"	B32D	1961		
41		"	601269	"	"	B32D	1961		
42		Sunbeam MF2B	TFD75806	BTH	UTIC	B32D	1965		
43		"	TFD75817	"	UTIC	B32D	1965		
44		"	TFD75827	"	UTIC	B32D	1965		
45		"	TFD75814	"	UTIC	B32D	1965		
46		"	TFD75821	"	UTIC	B32D	1965		
47		"	TFD75810	"	UTIC	B32D	1965		
48		Henschel Obus II	25231		CAMO	B36D	1980	1980	Ex-Braga7
49		"	25234		CAMO	B36D	1980	1980	Ex-Braga8
50	166	Caetano Efacec 190TR110	252025046		S.Caetano	B37D	3/1983	2000	
51	167	"	252026047		"	"	"		
52	168	"	252027048		"	"	"	2000	
53	169	"	252028049		"	"	"	2000	
54	170	"	252029050		"	"	"		
55	171	"	252030051		"	"	"		
56	172	"	252031052		"	"	"	2000	
57	173	"	252032053		"	"	"		
58	174	"	252033054		"	"	4/1984		
59	175	"	252034055		"	"	"		
60	176	"	252035056		"	"	"	2000	
61	177	"	252036057		"	"	"	2000	

FLEET NO	REG NO	CHASSIS	NO	ELECTRIC EQUIP	BODY	SEATS	NEW/ ACQU	OUT	NOTES
62	178	"	252037058		"	"	"	2000	
63	179	"	252038059		"	"	"		
64	180	"	252039060		"	"	"	2000	
65	181	"	252040061		"	"	"	2000	
66	182	"	252041062		"	"	"		
67	183	"	252042063		"	"	"	2000	
68	184	"	252043064		"	"	"		
69	185	"	252044065		"	"	"		
70	193	Caetano Efacec 175TL	252022043		"	AB41T	3/1985	2009	Ex-STCP 167 9/2003
71	165	Caetano Efacec 175TR110	52014035		"	B32D	5/1985		Ex-STCP 74 9/2003
75	85-IF-86	Solaris / Skoda Trollino III	7649		Solaris	B42D	2009		Bought demo 2009

Turning from the Avenida Emídio Navarro at Portagem is Coimbra's first trolleybus, number 21, whose fleet number followed on directly from Coimbra's last tramcar. This trolleybus was a Swiss-built Saurer 3TP and had Saurer's own B22D bodywork. The diminutive vehicle was built in 1948 in order to operate on the 6 route over the newly opened Santa Clara Bridge over the River Mondego through to the village of Pequeninos and then on to the Santa Clara monastery. This experimental route was the first in Portugal to be operated by trolleybuses. (A. Johnson)

Above: The same short wheelbase trolleybus but with its second body, built in 1972 by UTIC and at the same location at Portagem, is Saurer 3TP trolleybus 21. Behind the trolleybus is the spectacular, circular-towered end of the Art Nouveau Hotel Astoria. Travelling along the Avenida Emídio Navarro on the eastern bank of the River Mondego is a well-laden Nissan Diesel 7 ton lorry. (P. M. Photography)

Below: Preserved in the Coimbra Transport Museum at Alegria is trolleybus 22. This is the second of the pair of Saurer 3TP and was rebodied with a Salvador Caetano B28D body in 1974. It was officially withdrawn in 1987. It had been lovingly restored and placed in the museum some time earlier. It is parked in the museum in August 1984, suggesting that it had not been used after its final repaint for several months. (D. R. Harvey)

Above: An overview of a town centre can help enormously in locating various features in relation to one another. One of the 23–28 class of Park Royal-bodied Sunbeam MF2s stands in the small bus station at Largo da Portagem, (Place of the Gateway). Beyond the Avenida Emídio Navarro, which runs across the photograph from left (south) to right (north), is the Santa Clara Bridge over the River Montego. Soon after it was opened in 1947 it was used by the 6 trolleybus route to reach Santa Clara Monastery. The large statue is of Joaquim António de Aguiar, Prime Minister of Portugal between 1808 and 1817. (Commercial Postcard)

Below: Working on the 5 route to San Jose along the Avenida Emídio Navarro is trolleybus 23. This was the first of the 23–28 class Sunbeam MF2s with its original Park Royal B40D bodywork dating from 1951. Except for the deep sliding saloon ventilators, strong echoes of standard British ideas on body design were a characteristic of these single-deckers. In the far distance, behind the trolleybus, is the Estação Nova Railway Station, which is the main station for regional trains. It was opened in 1885 and has a fine decorative frontage with a central clock tower. Alongside the parked Volkswagen 'Beetle' is the side of the Hotel Astoria. (D. R. Harvey Collection)

Above: Being overtaken by a Peugeot 504 taxi in the old town is 1951 Sunbeam MF2Bs trolleybus 23. The appearance of 23, the first of the 23–28 class, was transformed when it was rebodied by Salvador Caetano in 1974, already 24 years old with a strikingly modern-looking B33D body. This re-bodying extended the life of the vehicle by nineteen years until it was finally withdrawn in June 1993. The somewhat slab-sided body was typical of the Caetano bodies built in the 1970s with a single-piece ovoid-shaped windscreen design that was to be repeated when the front of the UTIC bodies of the 1965 Sunbeam MF2Bs were rebuilt in mid-career. (P. M. Photography)

Below: Six further trolleybuses were delivered to Coimbra and entered service in 1951 and were numbered 23–28. They were Wolverhampton-built Sunbeam's MF2Bs that were fitted with single deck bodywork built by Park Royal, with 40 seats and room for 35 standing passengers. In order to enable them to be operated by just the driver, they had an overhang of 8.25 feet beyond the front axle, allowing the entrance door to be opposite the driver. To cope with the steep gradients of the Coimbra system, they were fitted with 125 horsepower 600-volt motors. On 10 August 1966, 24 operates on the 5 route in Rua Olimpio Nicolau Rui Fernandes at the junction with Praça De Maio, under the watchful eye of the traffic policeman standing on his dais. (R. Symons)

Above: On 10 August 1966 Sunbeam's MF2B 25 is being watched by the be-hatted newspaper seller as it stands parked and empty. The attractive the low mounted Park Royal bodywork on these six-strong batch of single-deckers was characterised by the heavy guttering above the half drop saloon windows. These served as both guttering to deflect the heavy spring rainfall and as sunshades in the heat of the summer. Somehow the original Park Royal bodywork and the large low pressure front tyres gave the six Sunbeam MF2Bs a slightly racy look. It had been working on the 5 route to San Jose at the south eastern extremity of Coimbra's trolleybus system. (R. Symons)

Below: Trolleybus 25, a 1951 Sunbeam's MF2B works on the route to the University. It is at Portagem when travelling south along the Avenida Emídio Navarro. Behind the trolleybus is the curved end of Art Nouveau Hotel Astoria. It carries a Salvador Caetano B34D body plus standees, with which it was rebodied in 1974. The deep windowed five-bay bodywork had a front entrance (which enabled the driver to collect fares) and a rear exit. Just behind the rear doors are five inset steps that enabled mechanics to get to the trolleypoles and the roof-mounted electrical equipment. (P. M. Photography)

Above: About to pass the Coimbra Transport Museum in the dual-carriageway Avenida Emídio Navarro, alongside the River Mondego in Alegria, is Salvador Caetano-rebodied Sunbeam's MF2B trolleybus 26. It is travelling towards Largo Da Portagem Bus Station on 5 August 1984 before negotiating the narrow shop-lined Rua Ferreira Borges in the City Centre. From the side view, the roof mounted electrical equipment is more exposed than on the original Park Royal bodies, which had trolley shrouds. (D. R. Harvey)

Below: Sunbeam MF2B trolleybus 27 was built in 1951 and still had its original Park Royal B32D body when travelling along the tree-lined dual-carriageway in Avenida Emídio Navarro near to the Alegria Transport Museum on 10 August 1966. It is about to pass a couple of Volkswagen 'Beetles', a pair of French-built Simca Arondes and a Fiat 600 just in front of the Triunfo advertisement. (R. Symons)

Above: Picking up passengers at the bus shelters at the entrance to the Santa Clara Bridge is trolleybus 28, the last of the rebodied 1951 Sunbeam MF2Bs. It has only recently been rebodied by Salvador Caetano, with a B34D body layout as it still had the trolley shrouds on the cant rail, easily identifiable with the almost inevitable advertisement for Mabor car tyres. With the Hotel Astoria that opened in 1926 in the background, a grossly overloaded flatbed lorry passes the rear of the trolleybus as it travels south eastward along the Avenida Emídio Navarro in 1975. (P. M. Photography)

Opposite above: In 1954, three more trolleybuses were delivered to SMC in order to augment the small eight-strong fleet. These were BUT LETB1s with BTH equipment and were supplied with the last Park Royal bodies built for Coimbra. The bus is quite new as it still sports its circular BUT badge on the front panel. This body design was virtually identical to those supplied on the 1951 Sunbeam MF2Bs. Parked in the depot yard is trolleybus 31, the last of the trio. The bodywork design was slightly spoilt by the bottom of the driver's signalling window being in line with the bottom of the saloon windows. The major design difference from the earlier Park Royal bodies was at the rear, where a double thickness pillar was added in order to brace the overhang and rear platform immediately behind the rear axle. The thicker front pillar behind the cab and front entrance contained the electrical cables taking the power from the trolleybooms to the forward-mounted traction motors. (D. R. Harvey Collection)

Below: The nearside rear view of the Park Royal bodywork on BUT LETB1 trolleybus 31 shows the trolley retrievers mounted on the lower rear panels. It is parked at the Roman Aqueduto de Sao Sebastiao in August 1967 when working on the 5 route. This trolleybus route did not follow any previous tram route and went from Aqueduto for about 2 miles to Liceu at the eastern end of the trolleybus system. (R. Symons)

Above: Trolleybus 31, a 1954 BUT LETB1 with a Park Royal B32D body, descends Rua Ferreira Borges in Coimbra on Sunday 5 August 1984, when it was over 90°F with a blazing sun and little shade. When walking down the narrow hill with its many tourist shops, restaurants and bars, there was a solitary newsagent with a billboard outside stating in Portuguese that earlier in the day the great Welsh actor Richard Burton had died at his home in Céligny near Geneva in Switzerland from a brain haemorrhage at the age of 58. Although a semi-reformed alcoholic, it felt only right to go to a bar in order to toast his memory and passing with a large Super Bock draught lager. (D. R. Harvey)

Below: Travelling down the hill towards Praça de Maio and the Roman Catholic Cathedral of Igreja de Santa Cruz in the Rua Ferreira Borges on 5 August 1984 is trolleybus 32. This Leyland-built BUT LETB1 trolleybus had a UTIC B32D dated from 1958. The bodywork design was clearly derived from the previous eight Park Royal-bodied trolleybuses. Over 20 years later this attractive street would become pedestrianised due to its narrowness for vehicular traffic. (D. R. Harvey)

Above: Picking up a passenger on the Santa Clara Bridge over the River Montego, with the city of Coimbra climbing up the Alcáçova Hill, surmounted with the sixteenth century Holy Cross Monastery in the distance, is trolleybus 32. This was the first of the 32–36 class of UTIC-bodied BUT LETB1, which had BTH electrical equipment. They were fitted with small Volkswagen petrol engines at the rear of the chassis in order for them to manoeuvre away from the overhead when required. The trolleybus is working on the 6 route to Santa Clara.(D. R. Harvey Collection)

Below: Turning right into the Rua Olimpio Nicolau Rui Fernandes from the Praça De Maio is BUT LETB1 trolleybus 32. Behind is part of Coimbra's imposing police station. Just visible at the top of the rear window of its UTIC bodywork are three hinges, showing that the window could be used as an emergency exit in the event of an accident. On the other side of the road is parked a Fiat 127 and a Renault 5, which due in part to the then somewhat impoverished Portuguese economy, were typical of the affordable cars available in the country in the 1970s. (P. M. Photography)

Above: The trolleybus station at Largo da Portagem is just visible on the right as 33, the second of the five 1957-built BUT LETB1s with a UTIC B32D body travels along Avenida Emídio Navarro at Portagem working the 5 route to Estádio. Behind the trolleybus, towering over the following Ford Cortina estate car is the wonderful Art Nouveau-styled Hotel Astoria. This is a superb piece of 1920s architectural 'rhubarb' standing in the narrow triangular site between the main riverside road and the Rua da Sota. It is just as impressive on the inside with a Charles Rennie Mackintosh-Style Art Nouveau entrance lobby. (P. M. Photography)

Below: Single-decker UTIC B32D bodied BUT LETB1 trolleybus 33 works the 5 route with Estadio displayed on the destination blind. The trolleybus is standing in front of a school with a small bell in the structure over the main entrance porch. This trolleybus was to be withdrawn in December 1991 and, like all of 32–35 batch of vehicles, was never re-bodied. (P. M. Photography)

Above: Standing at the bus shelters and about to travel over the Santa Clara Bridge on its way to Santa Clara on the 6 route is BUT LETB1 trolleybus 34. By now the UTIC bodywork had lost its trolleybus shrouds along with any revenue usually accrued from the normal advertisement for Mabor tyres. Behind it is the Hotel Astória, which was designed in pure Parisian Art Nouveau style on a corner flat-iron lot in 1919. It boasted an iconic façade with eclectic detailing, typical of the period. It took seven years to complete and when it finally opened in 1926 it was the first hotel in Portugal to offer in-room telephones for its guests. (P. M. Photography)

Below: BUT LETB1 trolleybus 34 crosses the Santa Clara Bridge towards Santa Clara whilst working on the 6 route. Behind the trolleybus, on the northern side of the River Mondego, is the city of Coimbra with the 16th century Holy Cross Monastery and part of Coimbra's famous University on the Alcáçova Hill. Travelling towards the distant city is a very early post-war Fiat 508C saloon car. Following the trolleybus is a Bedford O type lorry. (D. R. Harvey Collection)

Above: Parked up in the trolleybus depot yard in 1972 is trolleybus 35. This was the last of the batch built in 1957 with UTIC B32D bodywork. All Coimbra's tram, trolleybus and bus fleets wore the very smart and immaculately maintained municipal colours of yellow lower panels, white window surrounds and a grey roof. 35 has, like all of Coimbra's vintage trolleybuses, a pair of triple chrome corner bumpers. Unlike many of this make, it has managed to retain its BUT badge on the front apron. (D. R. Harvey Collection)

Below: 1961-vintage 36, a UTIC B32D-bodied BUT LETB1, is being followed by Sunbeam MF2B 46 in the Rua Ferreira Borges in August 1984. 36 is about to leave the trolleybus stop in the Praça de Maio in front of the Igreja de Santa Cruz Catholic Cathedral. Both of these vehicles were rebuilt with single piece Salvador Caetano-style windscreens in the mid-1970s, losing their trolley shrouds on the cantrail about at the same time. (D. R. Harvey)

Above: Travelling south eastwards along Avenida Emídio Navarro at Portagem and manoeuvring through the complex overhead is SMC's 37. This BUT LETB1 entered service in 1961 and had a UTIC B32D body based on the earlier Park Royal bodies built for Coimbra. It is being employed on the 5 route to Universidade. It was in service from February 1962 until December 1989. The bodywork was slightly different to earlier Park Royal bodies supplied to SMC as it had access steps to the roof on the thicker pillar just in front of the rear wheel arch. (P. M. Photography)

Below: The impressive 1926 Hotel Astoria towers over the Avenida Emídio Navarro as AEI-powered BUT LETB1 trolleybus 38 passes the hotel at Portagem having just left the forecourt of the Estação Nova Railway Station. It is working on the long, circular 3 route to Santo Antonio at the extreme north east of the trolleybus system via the Rua de Santa Teresa. This was one of five of the class to survive until January 1993. (P. M. Photography)

Above: Working on the 6 route at the bottom of the Rua Ferreira Borges in the Praça de Maio on 5 August 1984 is trolleybus 39. This 1961 BUT LETB1 had AEI electrics and had a UTIC B32D body. It is working on the 6 route from Santa Clara. The nineteenth century buildings, many with Juliette balconies and the decorative Azulejos tiling, stand around this square while on the extreme right are a number of open air restaurants protected with sunshades from the summer sunshine. (D. R. Harvey)

Below: Turning left into the Rua Ferreira Borges from the riverside Avenida Emídio Navarro at Portagem is BUT LETB139. Behind it is the prow of the Hotel Astória and the narrow Rua da Sota leading back to the old city centre. This 1961 vintage BUT LETB1 had a UTIC B32D and was one of the half dozen that had AEI electrical equipment rather than the previous batch that had BTH electrics. 39 is working on the 8 route and still retains its original two-piece windscreen. (D. R. Harvey Collection)

Above: Turning into the trolleybus station at Largo da Portagem is UTIC B32D bodied BUT LETB1 trolleybus 40. The cars parked on the right stand on the embankment of the River Mondego. The bus will then continue into the old town by way of the narrow Rua Ferreira Borges. These buses were capable of being one-man-operated, although frequently had a conductor on board. The front entrance and rear exit arrangement was of great value allowing for a good interior passenger flow. (D. R. Harvey Collection)

Below: Trolleybus 41 pulls away from the space of the Igreja de Santa Cruz Catholic Cathedral in the Praça de Maio at the bottom of Rua Ferreira Borges. It is 5 August 1984 when it was being used on the 8 route to Santo Antonio. By now 23 years old, the trolleybus is in remarkably original condition, even to the extent of retaining its chrome wheel nut rings; the only major alteration was the removal of the trolley-base shrouds. (D. R. Harvey)

Above: 41 is parked above the city centre when working on the 5 route. This BUT LETB1 had a two-door UTIC built B32D body whose design was more than just inspired by the earlier bodies supplied to SMC by Park Royal in 1954. The trolleybus is, as usual, well maintained and immaculately presented in the fleet livery of yellow, white and grey. One of the other excellent characteristics of the system was the tightly strung overhead wiring, which as in this case above the trolleybus, is taut and straight. (D. R. Harvey Collection)

Below: 42 was the first of the six Sunbeam MF2Bs built in 1966. These trolleybuses were actually built at Fallings Park factory of Guy Motors in Wolverhampton and had Guy chassis numbers, in this case TFD75806. They were the last trolleybus chassis to be built by Sunbeam who had constructed their previous trolleybuses some three and a half years earlier with an order for Bournemouth Corporation. The UTIC bodies were by this time a well-built if somewhat dated design, but did remain in service until November 1991. It is working on the Santa Clara route in the Avenida Santa De Bandeira on Wednesday 10 September 1966. (R. Symons)

Above: Waiting at the foot of the Rua Alexander Herculano is Sunbeam MF2B 42 with a BTH 125 hp motor. It was built with a UTIC B32D body and entered service in 1966. In mid-career, these trolleybuses were rebuilt with a single-piece ovoid-shaped windscreen of a rather uninspired design. The trolleybus is operating on the 1 route on 30 August 1986 and has come down from the part of the city that houses the ancient University of Coimbra. The University of Coimbra was founded in 1308 by King Dinis I. By 1537 the University was moved by King John III to the Coimbra Royal Palace, and expanded by 1544 to occupy the Coimbra Royal Palace. Since then, city life has revolved around the state-run university. For many decades, several colleges were established by the religious orders but these have all been absorbed into the present university. Visible from all over the city is the tall Baroque University Tower dating from between 1728 and 1733. (P. J. Thompson)

Below: The large open space of the Praça de Maio at the bottom of Rua Ferreira Borges was dominated by the Igreja de Santa Cruz Catholic Cathedral. On 5 August 1984, UTIC-bodied Sunbeam MF2B 43, which had entered service in 1966, picks up passengers at the stop in front of the Cathedral still sporting its original two piece windscreen. Parked on the left is a Pegaso J4 minibus that was built under license in Spain from a BMC J4. (D. R. Harvey)

Above: Sunbeam MF2B trolleybus 44, which was built in 1966 and was fitted with UTIC-bodied B32D body, still carries the triangular Sunbeam badge on the front panel. It is travelling along the tree-lined dual-carriageway Avenida Emídio Navarro towards Largo da Portagem when operating on the 10 route from Estádio. It is near to the Alegria Transport Museum when only a few months old on 10 August 1966 with the River Mondego embankment on the extreme right. It survived until February 1994 as one of the last pair of the class to remain in service. (D. R. Harvey)

Below: Manoeuvring around the turning circle at the Santa Clara terminus on the 6 route is Sunbeam MF2B 45. Although not required at this location, these trolleybuses had manoeuvring traction batteries carried beneath the rear transverse seat. Turning circles of this size were well within the capabilities of the specification of the Sunbeam MF2Bs as they could turn within a 60 ft radius. The dual door single-deck body had been built by UTIC with the capacity to carry up to 35 standing passengers in addition to the 32 occupying the available seats. This batch of trolleybuses were the last trolleybus chassis to be constructed by Sunbeam. (D. R. Harvey Collection)

Above: Travelling down Rua Ferreira Borges from Portagem on 4 August 1984 is UTIC-bodied Sunbeam MF2B trolleybus 46. By this date the original two-piece windscreen had been replaced by a cheaper, single ovoid-shaped windscreen, similar to those fitted to Salvador Caetano buses. This rebuilding might have stopped leaking and rattling but they were aesthetically devoid of a design that was harmonious to the rest of the UTIC body shape. (D. R. Harvey)

Below: Standing in front of the Renaissance and Baroque-styled Igreja de Santa Cruz Catholic Cathedral in the Praça de Maio on 5 August 1984 is Sunbeam MF2B 46.This was one of the 42–47 class bodied by UTIC with a B32D body that had entered service in 1966. The monastery and church were erected between 1132 and 1223 and having had Papal support during the thirteenth and fifteenth centuries became the centre of this extremely wealthy Portuguese diocese in the Coimbra area. The distant Rua Ferreira Borges is really congested with both local shoppers from Coimbra as well as many tourists who are slowing down the traffic including the two trolleybuses behind the Sunbeam. (D. R. Harvey)

Above: Passing over the long-abandoned tram tracks in the Rua Ferreira Borges on 4 August 1984 is trolleybus 50 (166), the first of the 1984 Caetano-190TR 110s with a Caetano B37D body, which was only five months old. The Rua Ferreira Borges was used only in the northwards direction when the daily services were operated. At the end of the daily services the trolleybuses had to travel in the reverse direction under police guard in order to reach the depot at Alegria. 150 is coming into the City Centre from Santa Clara. (D. R. Harvey)

Below: Passing Coimbra's central police station in the Rua Olimpio Nicolau Rui Fernandes is 51 (167), when only five months old. This 1984 batch of Caetano B37D bodied Caetano-190TR 110s were the first in the fleet to have registration plates of which 50–69 and 166–185 had non-matching registrations. The vehicles numbered 50–65 entered service throughout 1984 whereas 66–69 were stored for over four and a half years with the first three not being used until the autumn of 1987. Number 69 was only placed in service in July 1988. (D. R. Harvey)

Above: Leaving the Praça de Maio on 5 August 1984 is trolleybus 52 (168). It is being used on the 5 route. Although the Salvador Caetano bodywork of these 1984-built trolleybuses was somewhat small and box-like, these two-door bodied trolleybuses managed to squeeze in some 37 seated passengers. Although it was barely 11.30 am, this was a very hot Sunday and the open air restaurants and bars, one of which is on the right, were already becoming very busy. (D. R. Harvey)

Below: 54 (170) returns to Largo Da Portagem near to the Estação Nova Railway Station having worked on the circular 4 route from Cruz De Celas. These short wheelbase Caetano EFACAG trolleybuses were very manoeuvrable and were fitted with small diesel engines that were mounted behind the rear axle in order to move where diversions were required, or if there was a failure in the electrical overhead. They originally were 37-seaters but in order to get extra standee passengers on to the vehicle, the seating capacity was reduced to a B32D layout. (D. R. Harvey Collection)

Above: Parked in the Guarda Inglesa garage yard are three of the Caetano B37D bodied Efacec/Caetano 175TR 110 trolleybuses. 55 (171), 63 (179) and 58 (174) are parked against the wall of the maintenance building and face the distant entrance. In the first decade of the twenty-first century, there was a belated, albeit slight change of policy regarding the retention of trolleybuses in Coimbra and evidence of this was the painting of the lower body panels in pale blue. (D. R. Harvey Collection)

Below: About to enter the Praça Republica on its way back to Largo Da Portagem on 30 August 1986 is trolleybus 55 (171). This is a Caetano EFACAG trolleybus with a Caetano B37D body from the tree-lined Rua Lourenço de Almeida Azevedo. The 3 tram route had been one of the last two of Coimbra's tram services to be abandoned on St Valentine's Day 1980; the tarmaced-over tram tracks are just visible behind the trolleybus. (P. J. Thompson)

Above: 56 (172) leads identical Caetano EFACAG trolleybus, 63 (179), down the narrow Rua Ferreira Borges from the distant Largo Da Portagem. Both of these trolleybuses had Salvador Caetano B37D bodywork. Seen here on 5 August 1984, 56 is being used on the 5 route to São José; it was just four months old and would be withdrawn in 2000. (D. R. Harvey)

Below: Taking the quite tight turn in front of the Edificio Coimbra building on 29 August 1986 is trolleybus 57 (173). This Salvador Caetano-bodied EFACEG/Caetano 37-seater single-decker is being used on the 4 route. These short wheelbase trolleybuses were ideal for the tight turns and narrow streets in the centre of Coimbra but they were not long lived in the city. This was due in part to their lightweight construction but also because Coimbra's trolleybus system was subjected to being gradually run down between 1993 and 2001. A number of trolleybuses were included in this demise, though 57 was chosen to remain in service and still operates in 2019. (P. J. Thompson)

Above: Travelling down the Rua Olimpio Nicolau Rui Fernandes, with the outbound trolleybus overhead coming out of the Praça De Maio on the extreme right, is Caetano B37D bodied Caetano-190TR 110 with the fleet number 58 (174). It is 5 August 1984 and the trolleybus has just pulled out from the bus stop below the large letter S on the tall lamp standard, causing a queue of seven vehicles behind it. (D. R. Harvey)

Below: Trolleybus 59 (175) is squeezing past an illegally parked French-registered Alfa Romeo sports car on 5 August 1984 in the very busy but extremely narrow Rua Ferreira Borges. This one-man-operated Caetano-190TR 110 trolleybus had Salvador Caetano B37D bodywork and entered service in April 1984. It is operating on the 4 route and is going to Cruz De Celas in the upper part of the city. The appearance of these five bay construction bodies was rather spoilt by the wide body pillars between the windows. (D. R. Harvey)

Above: Also working on the circular 4 route to Cruz De Celas is trolleybus 60 (176), a 1984-built EFACEG/Caetano-190TR 110 with a Salvador Caetano body. It is loaded up at the bus stop in front of the Igreja de Santa Cruz Catholic Cathedral in the Praça De Maio with a full complement of passengers, including a very large number of standees. Parked in front of the Cathedral is a Renault 4 estate car and a more luxurious Citroen DS19 saloon. (A. Greaves)

Below: Waiting in the Largo Da Portagem Bus Station in August 1988 is 63 (179), one of the EFACEG/Caetano-190TR 110s that had entered service in November 1984. The large statue is of Joaquim António de Aguiar, the influential Portuguese Prime Minister who was in office at the end of the Peninsular Wars. Behind the trolleybus is the River Montego with the entrance of the Santa Clara Bridge just visible. The trolleybus driver, standing by the trolleybus cab, is taking a well-earned break having arrived at Portagem on the 8 route from Santa Antonio. (D. R. Harvey)

Above: Passing through Portagem is 63 (179), an EFACEG/Caetano-190TR 110 trolleybus. It is about to turn left into the bus terminus at Largo Da Portagem where it will terminate. Travelling in the opposite direction towards the railway station is one of the most popular medium sized cars in Portugal at the time; the Farina-designed Peugeot 504, which was in production from 1968 until 1983. Behind the trolleybus is the Hotel Astória and the narrow Rua da Sota leading back into the old town centre where located are the bars and restaurants of Coimbra as well as nightclubs and bars specialising in the famous Coimbran-style of Fado with its wonderful soul searching songs and guitar music. (D. R. Harvey)

Below: Travelling into the city on the 3 route along the Rua Olimpio Nicolau Rui Fernandes in August 1988 is EFACEG/Caetano 190TR 110 trolleybus 65 (181). This was the last of these 20-strong class of trolleybuses to enter service in 1984. It will go back to the city by way of a somewhat circuitous route via the railway station and the Mondego riverside embankment to Largo Da Portagem. (D. R. Harvey)

Above: Don't go to Coimbra on a Sunday as the trolleybuses do not operate! Neither are they accessible at the Guarda Inglesa garage. However, all was not in vain on Sunday 5 May 2019, as three unidentified 1985-built EFACEG/Caetano 175TR 110 trolleybuses were visible in the yard and had their lower skirt panels repainted orange in order to match the livery of the motorbus fleet. Even better was throughout the city much of the overhead was still intact and was in good, taut condition. (D. R. Harvey Collection)

Below: When new in Areosa depot yard, Oporto, in August 1985, as STCP's 167, this trolleybus was bought by Coimbra in September 2003 as an experiment to enliven the declining Coimbran trolleybus fleet. 70 (193) was built in March 1985; this EFACEG/Caetano 175TL trolleybus was the articulated version of the 190TR110 and had a Caetano AB41T body. The short wheelbase of these articulated trolleybuses gave them a humped, broken-back appearance. The experiment of using articulated trolleybuses in Coimbra was not a qualified success and 70 was taken out of service in 2009 after only six years' operating in the city. (D.R.Harvey)

Working on the 1 route is 71 (165), formerly numbered 74 in the Oporto trolleybus fleet. It is a EFACEG/Caetano 175TR 110 dating from May 1985 and was bought from STCP in September 2003 along with the acquisition of number 70 from the Coimbra fleet. This single trolleybus had a Caetano B32D body but was slightly shorter than its native Coimbran cousins. It is working on the 1 route between the Estação Nova and Universidade and was one of the two trolleybus services to survive in the city. (D. R. Harvey Collection)

Above: 75 (85-IF-86) is the solitary 'new' trolleybus that was bought in 2009 and is operating on the 4 route to Olivais. It is a Solaris Trollino T12 III with Skoda 210 kW induction motor traction motors. The body is a Polish-built Solaris three-doored one and has a low floor with a three door layout. It has an auxiliary diesel engine in order for it to travel 'off wire' where necessary. Bought to try out pollution-free transport, it is noticeable that no further trolleybuses of this type have entered service in Coimbra. (D. R. Harvey Collection)

Below: The only 'modern' trolleybus in the fleet is 75 (85-IF-86). This Solaris Trollino T12 III was a speculative purchase made in 2009. The low sleek lines of the three door Solaris body has a front entrance so that one-man-operation can be employed. The centre and rear doors are both used as exits. It is working near to the city centre at the Estação Nova railway station, having returned from Santo António dos Olivais near to University Hill to the east of the historic city of Coimbra. It is the home of many University of Coimbra's sites. (D.R.Harvey Collection)

Oporto

By some way, the largest trolleybus system in Portugal was the 125-strong fleet in Oporto. In January 1959, 20 BUT trolleybuses with UTIC bodywork, built under licence from Park Royal, took to the streets to link Oporto with Vila Nova de Gaia across the Dom Luis Bridge on services 33, 35 and 36. These replaced tram routes 13 and 14 and 3. This enabled access to Carcereira depot to be achieved for the trolleys, and three new trolleybus services 31, 32 and 37 also reached Santo Ovidio and Coimbroes. The trolleybuses were originally in a different livery of cherry red, cream and grey roofs.

In 1963, a further six BUT LETB1 numbered 21–26 were delivered with similar-looking Dalfa single-deck bodies but with three doors and only 20 seats. However they did have room to cater for 51 standees, so they had a B20T+51 layout.

Porto took delivery of 50 double-deck Lancias with Dalfa bodywork between 1967 and 1968; they were numbered 101–150 and originally used on routes 10 to Venda Nova, 11 to São Pedro da Cova, 12 to Gondomar and 29 to Travagem. All four routes started from Bolhao behind the main city centre market. The 50 Lancia 130 double-decker model was an Italian-built trolleybus produced from 1967 to 1968, which had two doors and two staircases. The electrical equipment was from CGE who provided 130 hp motors. The body, with 68 seats, was built by Dalfa. These trolleybuses were famously the last class of double-decker trolleybuses to enter service anywhere in the world and similarly were the last to be operated when withdrawn in March 1995. At the same time, in 1966, a single-deck version of the Lancia double-deckers, numbered 27–51, entered service with Dalfa B29D+47 standees and was built on the same chassis type.

The system thrived and quickly expanded from its inauguration in January 1959 with services across the River Douro to Vila Nova de Gaia. The routes to Venda Nova, São Pedro da Cova, and to Gondomar came next (see above) and two more routes were opened to Ermesinde and Travagem in1968. The trolleybuses were able to provide a cheap and reliable method of public transport and when more vehicles were required to begin to replace the original 1959 fleet of Leyland LETB1s, fifteen Caetano/Efacec 175TR110s with Caetano B31D bodies (60–74), were purchased, entering service in February 1983. Two years later, with the seeming intent by the management of STCP to encourage trolleybus operation in the Oporto, another ten new vehicles (160–169) were purchased. These were the articulated version of the previous fifteen vehicles and were Caetano/Efacec 175TR110s with Caetano AB41T bodies. Both batches of Caetano/Efacec single-deckers were, due to changes in policy, civil engineering work, and, being unnecessarily advanced, doomed to have short lives.

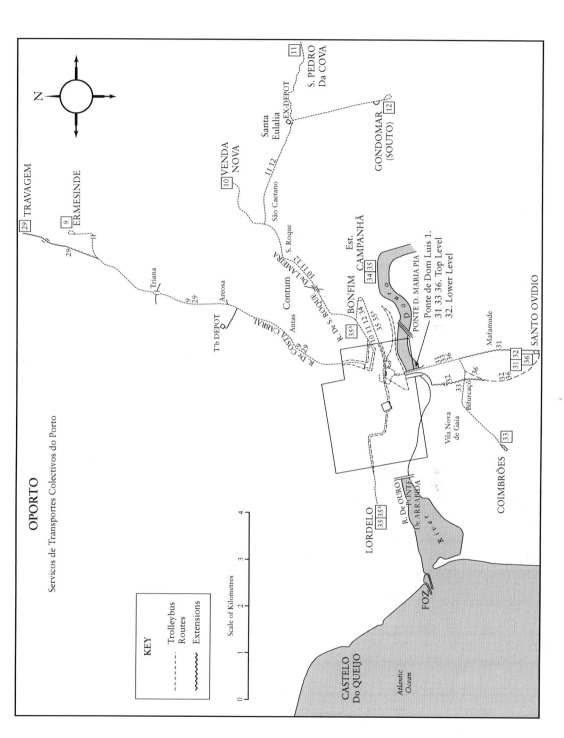

OPORTO

Serviços de Transportes Colectivos do Porto

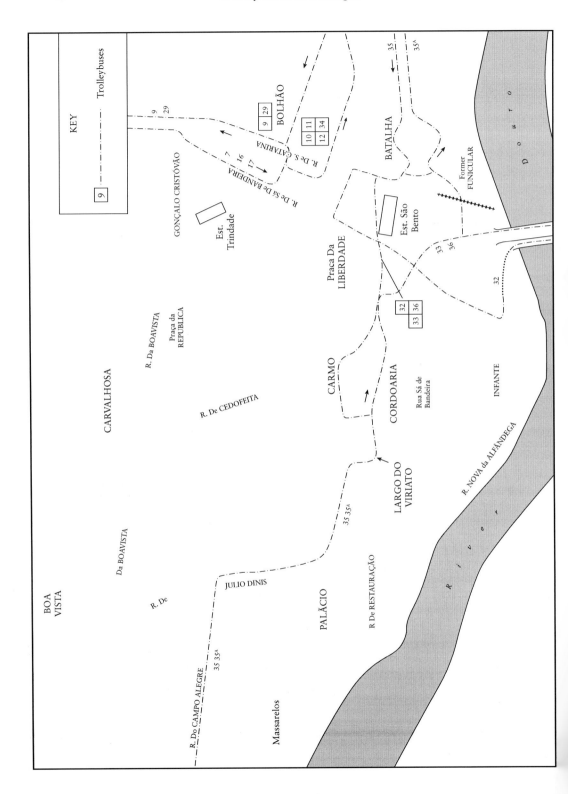

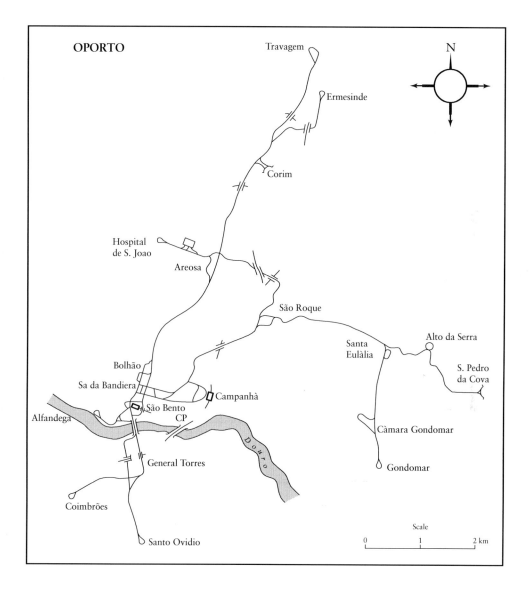

The demise of the Oporto trolleybus system is described earlier. After the bulk of the system was closed in March 1995, these last two batches of trolleybuses were the only ones to return to service. This was only until 27 December 1997 when the system was finally closed down.

Oporto Trolleybus Fleet

FLEET NO.	REG NO.	CHASSIS	NO.	ELECTRIC EQUIP	BODY	SEATS	NEW/ ACQU	OUT	NOTES
1	1	BUT LETB1	581471	MV 150 hp	UTIC	B32D +23	1/1959	1994	Preserved by STCP
2	2	"	581537	"	"	"	"	"	
3	3	"	581613	"	"	"	"	"	
4	4	"	581470	"	"	"	"	"	
5	5	"	581612	"	"	"	"	"	
6	6	"	581887	"	"	"	1959	"	
7	7	"	582072	"	"	"	"	"	
8	8	"	582159	"	"	"	"	"	
9	9	"	582226	"	"	"	"	"	
10	10	"	582227	"	"	"	"	"	
11	11	"	582529	"	"	"	"	"	
12	12	"	582160	"	"	"	"	"	
13	13	"	582561	"	"	"	"	"	
14	14	"	582635	"	"	"	"	"	
15	15	"	582717	"	"	"	5/1959	"	
16	16	"	582716	"	"	"	"	"	
17	17	"	582699	"	"	"	"	"	
18	18	"	582841	"	"	"	"	"	
19	19	"	582842	"	"	"	"	"	
20	20	"	582981	"	"	"	"	"	
21	21	BUT LETB1	S09901	MV 150 hp	UTIC	B20T + 51	1963	"	
22	22	"	S09902	"	"	"	"	"	
23	23	"	S09903	"	"	"	"	"	Preserved by STCP
24	24	"	S09904	"	"	"	"	"	Rebuilt to B26D
25	25	"	S09905	"	"	"	"	"	
26	26	"	S09906	"	"	"	"	"	
27	77	Lancia 103	001031	CGE 150 hp	Dalfa	B29D+47	1966	3/ 1995	
28	78	"	001032	"	"	"	"	"	

29	79	"	001033	"	"	"	"	"	
30	80	"	001034	"	"	"	"	"	
31	81	"	001035	"	"	"	"	"	
32	82	"	001036	"	"	"	"	"	
33	83	"	001037	"	"	"	"	"	
34	84	"	001038	"	"	"	"	"	
35	85	"	001039	"	"	"	"	"	
36	86	"	001040	"	"	"	"	"	
37	87	"	001041	"	"	"	"	"	
38	88	"	001042	"	"	"	"	"	
39	89	"	001043	"	"	"	"	"	
40	90	"	001044	"	"	"	"	"	
41	91	"	001045	"	"	"	"	"	
42	92	"	001066	"	"	"	"	"	
43	93	"	001067	"	"	"	"	"	
44	94	"	001068	"	"	"	"	"	
45	95	"	001069	"	"	"	"	"	
46	96	"	001070	"	"	"	"	"	
47	97	"	001071	"	"	"	"	"	
48	98	"	001072	"	"	"	"	"	
49	99	"	001073	"	"	"	"	"	
50	100	"	001074	"	"	"	"	"	
51	101	"	001975	"	"	"	"	"	
60	151	Caetano/ Efacec 175TR110	252000021	Efacec 223 hp	S.Caetano	B31D	1983	12/ 1997	
61	152	"	252001022	"	"	"		"	
62	153	"	252002023	"	"	"		"	
63	154	"	252003024	"	"	"		"	
64	155	"	252004025	"	"	"		"	
65	156	"	252005026	"	"	"		"	
66	157	"	252006027	"	"	"		"	
67	158	"	252007028	"	"	"		"	
68	159	"	252008029	"	"	"		"	
69	160	"	252009030	"	"	"		"	
70	161	"	252001031	"	"	"		"	
71	162	"	252011032	"	"	"		"	
72	163	"	252012033	"	"	"		"	
73	164	"	252013034	"	"	"		"	
74	165	"	252014035	"	"	"		"	

FLEET NO.	REG NO.	CHASSIS	NO.	ELECTRIC EQUIP	BODY	SEATS	NEW/ ACQU	OUT	NOTES
101	27	Lancia 140	001001	CGE 150 hp	Dalfa	H43/25D	1966	3/ 1995	
102	28	"	001002	"	"	"	"	"	
103	29	"	001003	"	"	"	"	"	
104	30	"	001004	"	"	"	"	"	
105	31	"	001005	"	"	"	"	"	
106	32	"	001006	"	"	"	"	"	
107	33	"	001007	"	"	"	"	"	
108	34	"	001008	"	"	"	"	"	
109	35	"	001009	"	"	"	"	"	
110	36	"	001010	"	"	"	"	"	
111	37	"	001011	"	"	"	"	"	
112	38	"	001012	"	"	"	"	"	
113	39	"	001013	"	"	"	"	"	
114	40	"	001014	"	"	"	"	"	
115	41	"	001015	"	"	"	"	"	
116	42	"	001016	"	"	"	"	"	
117	43	"	001017	"	"	"	"	"	
118	44	"	001018	"	"	"	"	"	
119	45	"	001019	"	"	"	"	"	
120	46	"	001020	"	"	"	"	"	
121	47	"	001021	"	"	"	"	"	
122	48	"	001022	"	"	"	"	"	
123	49	"	001023	"	"	"	"	"	
124	50	"	001024	"	"	"	"	"	
125	51	"	001025	"	"	"	"	"	
126	52	"	001026	"	"	"	"	"	
127	53	"	001027	"	"	"	"	"	
128	54	"	001028	"	"	"	"	"	
129	55	"	001029	"	"	"	"	"	
130	56	"	001030	"	"	"	"	"	
131	57	"	001031	"	"	"	"	"	
132	58	"	001032	"	"	"	"	"	
133	59	"	001033	"	"	"	"	"	
134	60	"	001034	"	"	"	"	"	
135	61	"	001035	"	"	"	"	"	
136	62	"	001036	"	"	"	"	"	
137	63	"	001037	"	"	"	"	"	

138	64	"	001038	"	"	"	"	"	
139	65	"	001039	"	"	"	"	"	
140	66	"	001040	"	"	"	"	"	
141	67	"	001041	"	"	"	"	"	
142	68	"	001042	"	"	"	"	"	
143	69	"	001043	"	"	"	"	"	
144	70	"	001044	"	"	"	"	"	
145	71	"	001045	"	"	"	"	"	
146	72	"	001046	"	"	"	"	"	
147	73	"	001047	"	"	"	"	"	
148	74	"	001048	"	"	"	"	"	
149	75	"	001049	"	"	"	"	"	
150	76	"	001050	"	"	"	"	"	
160	186	Caetano/ Efacec	252015036	Efacec 224 hp	S.Caetano	AB 41T	1985	"	
161	187	"	252016037	"	"	"	"	"	
162	188	"	252017038	"	"	"	"	"	
163	189	"	252018039	"	"	"	"	"	
164	190	"	252019040	"	"	"	"	"	
165	191	"	252020041	"	"	"	"	"	
166	192	"	252021042	"	"	"	"	"	
167	193	"	252022043	"	"	"	"	"	To SMTUC, Coimbra 70, 9/2003
168	194	"	252023044	"	"	"	"	"	
169	195	"	252024045	"	"	"	"	"	

This list is in fleet number rather than chronological order.

1-20 The first trolleybuses

Above: Turning from its parking spot to exit Areosa's trolleybus depot is Oporto's 1 (1), its first trolleybus, which dated from January 1959. The city's first batch of trolleybuses was numbered 1–20 and were BUT LETB1 chassis powered by a MV 150 hp motor. They had rather stylish UTIC B32D+23 bodies built under licence in Lisbon using Park Royal designs. This trolleybus was subsequently saved for preservation after it was withdrawn in 1991 and beautifully restored back into its original deep red and white livery with a grey roof. (D. R. Harvey Collection)

Below: Standing in Areosa depot yard is UTIC-bodied BUT LETB1 2 (2). Areosa trolleybus depot on 14 August 1990. Behind this trolleybus is 16 (16), another of the first batch of twenty BUT LETB1 trolleybuses numbered 1–20 that entered service on 3 May 1959 when the Oporto system opened. These were three tram replacement services, 33, 35 and 36, a route numbered 3, which allowed access to the other trolleybus depot at Carcereira, and three new trolleybus routes numbered 31, 32 and 37. (D. R. Harvey)

Above: Nearly all of Oporto's single-decker trolleybuses were garaged at the extensive open depot at Areosa. 3 (3), equipped with a Metro Vickers 150 hp motor, is parked at the outer edge of the huge yard's peripheral road in August 1985. The bodies for these trolleybus were built to a Park Royal design under licence and remained largely unchanged until their withdrawal in the early 1990s. However a handful were altered and trolleybus 3 was one of them. This involved the original fixed windscreens being replaced by ones that had bottom opening ventilators in order to cool down the driver in the hot summer months and also to improve air flow through the bus. (D. R. Harvey)

Below: The adoption of the yellow and white livery after the April 1974 Revolution somehow lessened the somewhat distinguished appearance of Oporto's trolleybus fleet. This detraction was continued when body panels were adorned by advertising panels. UTIC-bodied BUT LETB1 4 (4) is parked at Areosa depot on 14 August 1990 and has a blank section of its body panels left in undercoat prior to the fitment of a new advertisement. The long seven bay single-deck body design is quite well masked by the proportions of the saloon windows and there was a certain similarity to the 35 ft long Burlingham-bodies on the BUT RETB1s built for Glasgow in late 1958. Maybe it was the orange livery! (D. R. Harvey)

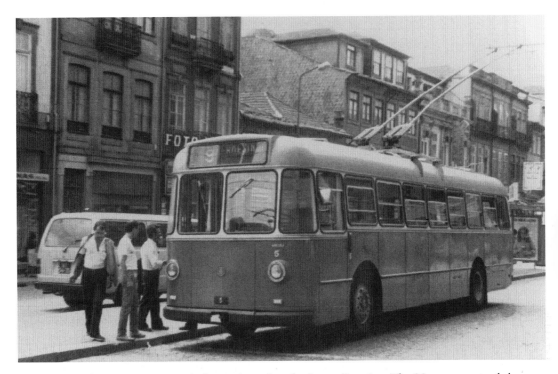

Above: The 9 route to Ermesinde terminated at the Santa Caterina. The 29 route covered the same route as the 9 as far as Corim but then continued on a two-mile extension to Travagem. These two routes were opened in November 1968 and were both operated by single-deckers. Trolleybus 5 (5), a 1958-vintage BUT LETB1, waits to start loading up with passengers in August 1985 when working on the Ermesinde route. This terminus, although in the city centre, was only a three-minute walk away from the more frequently photographed termini in Bolhao. (D. R. Harvey)

Opposite above: Working on a short section of the 9 route from Corim on the Ermesinde line, is a slightly battered-looking UTIC-bodied BUT LETB1 trolleybus 5 (5). The UTIC body has been repainted in the mid-1980s orange and white livery and has had the opening glass windscreen ventilators removed. The driving position and the rake of the steering wheel looks more comfortable on these British-built chassis when compared to the near horizontal steering wheels on the later Lancia trolleybuses. (P. Trotter)

Opposite below: The 5½-mile-long, single-decker-operated trolleybus 9 route to Ermesinde, to the northeast of Oporto, was opened on 17 November 1967. BUT LETB1 trolleybus 6 (6) stands at the terminus in the town near to the railway station with the water tower dominating the skyline. The town developed as initially a temporary settlement for the workers involved in the construction of the railway line in the second half of the nineteenth century from Oporto to Braga and the north. The town was also the junction of another railway line opened in 1887, which followed the River Douro Valley to Regua and terminated at Pocinho in the heart of the wine growing heartland of Northern Portugal. (D. R. Harvey Collection)

Above: Parked in the shade of the maintenance bay in the Areosa depot on 14 August 1990 is trolleybus 7 (7). The UTIC-body on this BUT LETB1 with its front entrance and rear exit has been modified with the lower opening windscreen. The high floor line and steep pair of steps into the saloon are visible through the somewhat narrow front doors. The thicker body pillar below the side destination box carries the electrical wiring from the trolleypoles to the MV 150 hp motor. It also has inset steps in order to gain access to the trolley gantry and the trolleypoles. (D. R. Harvey)

Below: Standing in front of 126 (52), one of the Dalfa-bodied Lancia double-deck trolleybuses in the Areosa depot yard in August 1985, is 1958-vintage single-decker 8 (8). This UTIC-bodied BUT LETB1 is still painted in its original red, white and grey livery and still retains its original windscreen layout. One of the recurring problems with the platform glazing were the curved side windows. These were prone to breaking and on some of these trolleybuses were replaced by Perspex windows, which could craze in the summer heat. It was not a long-lived experiment! (D. R. Harvey)

Above: On 14 August 1990, Oporto BUT LETB1 single-decker 9 (9) is parked along with other trolleybuses around the edge of the huge Areosa depot yard. It has its trolleybooms pulled down awaiting its next journey into the streets of the city. This trolleybus carries a large advertisement for Tudor car and traction batteries on the side panels on the UTIC body. Noticeable are the deep half-drop opening saloon windows, ideal for the hot Portuguese summers. (D. R. Harvey)

Below: Standing near to the Santa Caterina terminus in the Rua de Sa De Bandeira are a pair of single-deck UTIC-bodied BUT LETB1s. Working on the long 29 route to Travagem to the north of the city centre is 11 (11) sporting opening windscreen ventilators, while behind it is the unmodified 4 (4). This trolleybus is working on the 9 route to Ermesinde, which was a direct replacement for a tram route that had been converted to trolleybus operation on 17 September 1967. The 29 service was a new extension opened on 17 November 1968. Both of these two services had to be operated by single-deck trolleybuses due to a low bridge crossing the route at Triana. (D. R. Harvey Collection)

Above: The row of UTIC-bodied BUT LETB1s are parked around the edge of Areosa depot yard on 14 August 1990. The ticket machine is visible through the driver's windscreen on BUT LETB1 12 (12), showing that these large UTIC B32D+23 bodied trolleybuses were used as o-m-o vehicles. 12 is carrying the large side panel somewhat ubiquitous advertisement for Mabor car tyres. These were elegant-looking trolleybuses whose design was slightly spoilt by the exposed trolley gantry on the roof. (D. R. Harvey)

Opposite above: Parked in Areosa depot yard on Tuesday 14 August 1990 and awaiting repair work is UTIC-bodied BUT LETB1 13 (13), and Dalfa-bodied Lancia single-decker 34. Although only eight years separates their entry into service, the Park Royal-inspired UTIC bodywork on 13 (built in 1958) looks positively old-fashioned when compared to the angular lines of the body on 1966-vintage 34. The Lancia would remain in service until the closure of the Oporto trolleybus system in March 1995, whereas the BUT was not so lucky and was withdrawn a couple of years earlier having been reconfigured to a B26D interior layout. (D. R. Harvey)

Below: Parked behind a similar trolleybus (7) in the large Areosa trolleybus yard is 14 (14), on Tuesday 14 August 1990. Certainly these trolleybuses did not belong to the low-floor era of vehicles with two deep steps into the saloon and a rather narrow front door. The latter was very useful as it only allowed one passenger at a time to pay while allowing the driver to control the entering passengers. The contemporary Glasgow Burlingham-bodied BUT RETB1s had a similar layout. Conversely, the narrow entrance made for even slower loading. Swings and roundabouts! (D. R. Harvey)

Above: Waiting in 'its natural environment' is BUT LETB1 trolleybus 15 (15). Its UTIC body appears to have more than its official complement of 26 seated passengers, which was six less than when it was built. To compensate for this reduction in seats the number of standee straphanger passengers was increased from 23 to officially 36 but by the look of this trolleybus even more have been squeezed on board. 15 stands at the trolleybus terminus of the busy 9 route to Ermesinde in August 1988, showing how only one passenger at a time could enter the vehicle and pay the driver. This trolleybus terminus in the city centre was typical of so many termini around the world, as it loaded up in a somewhat out-of-the-way back street before emerging onto its long main route out of town. (D. R. Harvey)

Opposite above: Leaving the Santa Catarina terminus in August 1985 and passing an ice cream vendors ice box is trolleybus 16 (16). This UTIC-bodied BUT LETB1 is turning left into Rua de Santo Caterina over the typical cobbled streets of central Oporto with a backdrop of characteristic nineteenth century three- and four-storey buildings. The well-laden trolleybus is working on the 7-mile-long 9 route to Ermesinde and is still in its original red and white livery. (D. R. Harvey)

Below: The long trolleypoles on the 1-20 class are evident on the Oporto BUT LETB1 waiting at the Santa Catarina terminus before beginning its next tour of duty on the 9 route to Ermesinde. 17 (17), has a UTIC B26D plus standee capacity, which it would need for the busy 9 route. Just beyond the Areosa trolleybus depot there was a low railway bridge at Triana. The necessary height restriction on both the 9 and 29 routes precluded the use of double-deckers on these two services, which would have allowed for a greater number of passengers to be carried in the peak periods. (D. R. Harvey Collection)

UTIC-bodied BUT LETB1 trolleybus 18 (18) is parked in front of identical 2 (2), in Areosa depot yard on 14 August 1990. By now the 1-20 class of trolleybuses were well over 32 years old and while seemingly in better condition than the newer Dalfa-bodied Lancia single-deckers, they were due for replacement with little sign of renewal with new vehicles. They had a hard life pounding the cobbled setts of Oporto and had been a very sound investment in 1958 for STCP. (D. R. Harvey)

22-26 Three door BUT LETB1s

Above: 22 (22) is working on the 33 route to Coimbões, part of Vila Nova de Gaia. The 21–26 batch of BUT LETB1 had UTIC B20T bodies with the extra capacity of 51 standing passengers. Delivered in 1963, it was equipped with a Metro-Vic 150 hp motor. Unlike the previous 1958 batch of twenty BUTs, these trolleybuses were equipped with trolley base shrouds, which usually carried advertisements, in this case for Mabor car tyres. (D. R. Harvey Collection)

Below: BUT LETB1 23 (23), when new in 1963, is posed on the cobbles with the Praça da Liberdade behind it facing the famous São Bento Railway Station, noted for its wonderful azulejos-lined booking hall in the Praça Almeida Garrett. The trolley shrouds hiding the trolley gantry tidy up the appearance of the trolley bus. The inset steps to the roof and the overhead were something of an exercise in mountaineering as they were somewhat haphazardly laid out. The three-door layout of the UTIC bodywork had a narrow front entrance as was the centre exit. The double-width rear exit doors enabled passengers to quickly leave the trolleybus. (D. R. Harvey Collection)

Above: From the early 1980s, STCP began to put on one side vehicles that belonged to classes that were due for withdrawal. Many trams, buses and trolleybuses were stored at the now sadly demolished tram depot at Boa Vista where they languished under cover gathering dust for many years. To the credit of the company, all of the stored vehicles were lovingly restored back to their original condition. 23 (23) of 1963, parked in Massarelos depot, is back to its original condition with opening windscreen ventilators and trolley shrouds restored, though lacking the saloon guttering. It does look like it has just been delivered to STCP. (D. R. Harvey Collection)

Opposite above: The second batch of BUT LETB1 numbered just six trolleybuses, which were numbered 21–26 and all entered service in 1963. They had triple-door UTIC 20-seater bodywork with floor space for another 51 standing passengers. The UTIC bodywork, although derived from the bodywork on the 1–20 batch, somehow lacked the subtlety of the earlier design, having a flatter frontal aspect, which gave them a lower and yet less sleek appearance. By this date, the guttering over the saloon windows had been removed, which did not improve their appearance. 24 (24) is parked in front of its twin, 25 (25), in the parking area around the edge of Areosa depot yard in August 1985. (D. R. Harvey)

Below: 26 (26) is being used on the inbound 29 route to Bolhao. The second batch of UTIC bodied BUT LETB1s were only six in number and with their three doors and standee arrangement for 51 passengers were neither as popular or as well used as the 1–20 batch of two doored single-decker trolleybuses. One aspect of their design, which was retrospectively fitted to some of the earlier vehicles, was the small outward-opening ventilator window at the bottom of the windscreen to aid ventilation for the driver in the hot Portuguese summers. Perversely, it's the one nearest the platform that is open on trolleybus 26. (D. R. Harvey Collection)

27-51 Lancia single-deckers

Above: 29 (79) is near to the Santa Catarina terminus in the Oporto City Centre when operating on the 29 route to Travagem. This Italian-built Lancia 103 chassis had Portuguese CGE 150 hp motors but its Italian origins could be identified by the artillery-spoked front wheels, which were typical features of heavy commercial vehicles emanating from Italy. These powerful trolleybuses with their 130hp motors also had regenerative braking in order to cope with stresses of Oporto's steep hills. (D. R. Harvey Collection)

Opposite above: Seen from a bedroom in the Hotel Império into Batalha Square in August 1988 are two of the Lancia 103 two axle 11 metre long single deckers with Dalfa B29D+47 standee passengers. On the right is 30 (80), working on the 36 route to Santo Avidio via the top level of the Ponte de Dom Luis I over the River Douro, while parked next to the bus shelters is 45 (95), which has just arrived in Batalha and will sit next to the shelter for another ten minutes. (D. R. Harvey)

Below: Parked outside the 1960s Banco Portuguese building, later to become the Porto Royal Bridges Hotel, is one of the batch of 25 two-door Dalfa-bodied Lancia single-decker number 31 (81). It is waiting to resume its duties on the 36 route to Santo Ovidio on the southern side of the River Douro. Behind it is the famous A Braziliera restaurant and coffee house in Rua de Sá da Bandeira. It has a remarkable Art Deco façade, with the magnificent sunshade of iron and glass over the front entrance. (P. M. Photography)

Above: Parked in Areosa depot is Lancia single-decker 32 (82) on 14 August 1990. Compared to the earlier British-built trolleybus chassis operated in Oporto, the entrance and exit steps are much shallower due to the lower interior floor line of the vehicles. The Dalfa bodies had the overhead gantry concealed beneath a shapely streamlined box that looked a little like a luggage top-box that could be attached to a car roof. (D. R. Harvey)

Below: Parked in front of the wonderful A Braziliera cafeteria is Lancia trolleybus 33 (83). Located in Rua de Sá da Bandeira in the middle of Baixa do Porto, the café was opened on May 4, 1903, surprisingly it's one of the first coffee houses to open in Portugal. The Dalfa-bodied trolleybus is out of service as it is not showing a destination and has no passengers. Dalfa was a Portuguese body builder who originally specialised in van bodies but from the late 1950s built a considerable number of bus bodies especially for operators in the Oporto area. (D. R. Harvey Collection)

Coming off the lower level of the Ponte de Dom Luis I from the area of riverside port caves in Vila Nova da Gaia, on its way back to the city centre is Lancia single-decker 34 (84). The trolleybus is passing through the archway on the Oporto bank with the marble plaque, which has the inscription PONTE LUIS I above it. The Dom Luís I Bridge is a double-deck metal arched bridge that spans the River Douro between the cities of Porto and Vila Nova de Gaia. Begun in 1881, the upper deck was completed on 30 October 1886. Exactly two years later the lower level was also completed. The span is 192 yards long and stands 148 feet above the river. The trolleybus is working on the 32 route to Santo Ovidio on the lower route via Bifurcaçõ. It is before the class had their mid-life overhauls in the early 1980s when the opening ventilators in the windscreen of these Dalfa-bodied vehicles were removed and replaced by fixed panes, a move not popular with the suddenly perspiring trolleybus drivers. (D. R. Harvey Collection)

Above: In August 1985, Lancia single-decker 35 (85), stands in the Areosa trolleybus depot yard. Having had its mid-life body overhaul a few years earlier, this trolleybus has by now lost its opening windscreen ventilators, which have been replaced by single panes of glass thus producing a slightly deeper windscreen. Through this is revealed in the driver's cab the almost vertical steering column. Although the main saloon body pillars of the Dalfa bodywork are vertical, the angled windows adjacent to both the entrance and the exit are a pleasant detail that enhanced the appearance of these single-deckers. (D. R. Harvey)

Opposite above: Leaving the Praça da Batalha in August 1988 with the backdrop on the front of the cinema for Sylvester Stallone's new film 'Rambo III', is the red, white and grey painted trolleybus 36 (86). The Lancia single-decker is working on the 32 route to Santo Ovidio by way of the more circuitous route through Vila Nova de Gaia over the lower deck of the Ponte de Dom Luis I. This route would succumb to motorbuses in July 1993 thus abandoning the southern section of Oporto's trolleybus system. (D. R. Harvey)

Below: Leading a line of three Lancia 103s with Dalfa B29D+47 bodies in the Areosa depot yard in August 1985 is 37 (87). This trolleybus had recently been rebuilt with a pair of fixed windscreens and at the same time had been repainted in the new yellow and white livery. The two red and white painted Lancias behind 37 have yet to be overhauled and retain the opening section in the lower part of the windscreen. (D. R. Harvey)

Above: Climbing up the steep hill in Rua with the Praça Almeida Garrett behind it is BUT LETB1 38 (38) on 31 January. Behind the buildings on the left and in a cutting below the level of this busy retail city centre street are the platforms of the Estação São Bento via Bifurcaçõ. Trolleybus 38 is travelling towards the Praça da Batalha working on the 36 route from Santo Ovidio. It was because the steep hills, like this one in Oporto, that the trolleybuses required their powerful 150 hp CGE motors. The trolleybus was new in 1966 and with its silver painted wheels, looked in pristine condition. (D. R. Harvey Collection)

Above: Entering Batalha in August 1984 is Dalfa-bodied Lancia 103 type single-decker 40 (90). It is running back to Areosa trolleybus depot having completed its work for the day. The prominent Lancia badge on the front red painted panel is a reminder that these 25 single-deckers as well as the 50 Lancia double-deckers were ordered when the British trolleybus manufacturers at BUT and Sunbeam had all but ceased building new chassis. This left STCP no option but to look elsewhere in order to purchase new trolleybuses. The combined order for 75 of what proved to be quite splendid Italian-built Lancia single and double-decker trolleybuses was the largest ever placed by a Portuguese operator. (D. R. Harvey)

Opposite below: Coming into the north side of the Praça do Marques de Pombal from the Rua da Costa Cabral is Dalfa-bodied, two-door Lancia103 type single-decker trolleybus 39 (89). On 22 August 1987, this vehicle is working the 9 service and is returning back to Bolhao city centre from Ermesinde. This route travels through a suburban tree-lined oasis of parkland, which is lined with buildings that date back to the nineteenth century and surround the square. (P. J. Thompson)

Above: In August 1984, Lancia single-deck trolleybus, 41 (91), is parked with its trolleybooms down in Praça da Batalha in front of the then Cinema Batalha. It was showing a 1984 Italian comedy film "Lui è peggio di me" ("He is worse than me"), which was directed and also starred Adriano Celentano, an Italian vocalist, musician, producer, comedian, actor and film director. The Cinema Batalha originally opened on 29 February 1908 but was completely rebuilt with an Art Deco-inspired design, reopening on 3 June 1947 as a four-storey building. It had a basement and a recessed first-floor. The remaining floors jetty above the ground floor. The cinema included two auditoriums, one with 950 seats and one smaller cinema with 135 seats. It had several bars, a terrace restaurant and lounges on each floor. This imposing concrete structure dominates the one side of the Praça da Batalha opposite the nineteenth century French Renaissance-styled Hotel Império. The cinema closed in 2003 but after much discussion was re-opened as a major cultural and concert venue in 2006. (D. R. Harvey)

Opposite above: Speeding up the steep gradient in Avenida de Dom Afonso Henriques, where its powerful CGE 150 hp motor would be most appreciated, is Dalfa B29D bodied Lancia 103 single-decker 43 (93). The trolleybus navigates this hill from Estação São Bento, in the Praça Almeida Garretts (Oporto's main railway station, which can be seen in the distance at the bottom of the hill), to the Avenida de Vimara Perez and on to the top deck of the Ponte de Dom Luis I. It will then cross the Rover Douro by way of this spectacular crossing point some 148 feet above the river. (P. J. Thompson)

Below: 43 (93), negotiates almost as many pedestrians in the road as normal road vehicles as it passes down the Rua de Sá da Bandeira. This by now rebuilt Lancia 103 single-decker is working towards the famous A Braziliera restaurant and coffee house before travelling on to the Praça Almeida Garrett and the railway station at São Bento. It is working on the 36 route to Santa Ovidio by way of the lower section of the Ponte de Dom Luis I and will travel along the quayside of the River Douro in Vila Nova da Gaia, passing the moored port barrel wine carried from the Upper Douro Valley by sailing barges, and the many famous port caves owned by such long established companies such as Sandeman, Taylors, Calem and Grahams. (D. R. Harvey)

Above: Sunday 25 March 1973 was a typical rainy day in Porto (remember 'warm wet winters, hot dry summers'). At the entrance to the Praça da Batalha is trolleybus 44 (94), a Lancia 103 with a Dalfa B29D body, parked in front of the statue of King Pedro V of Portugal. The statue was unveiled in 1866 and is mounted on a tall elaborately embossed pedestal only five years after the square was first urbanised. The body of the trolleybus had angular main pillars, which not only made them look better but also added to the vehicles structural integrity. The trolleybus is still in its original livery and unmodified condition. (F. Hornby)

Below: The sign of 'things to come' and an ominous portent for the Porto trolleybuses! In Praça da Batalha, Lancia trolleybus 45 (95) has just arrived in the square and is parked alongside the cinema complex. It is August 1988 and the 33 service would only last for another five years. The trolleybus is being overtaken by 1003 (OT-51-18), an articulated Volvo B10M-55, with a CAMO AB37T dating from July 1983 and was withdrawn in January 2005, ten years after the trolleybus was scrapped. (D. R. Harvey)

Above: If to drive a car over the upper deck of the Ponte de Dom Luis I was a superb experience, to ride in a trolleybus was magnificent! Alas the top deck is now pedestrianised and the Oporto Metro D Line tram, which was inaugurated on 18 September 2005, is now the only traffic that operates on the top level of the bridge. The bridge is a double-deck iron arch structure that spans the River Douro some 279 feet above the water level. Lancia 103 type 45 (95) drives over the bridge travelling toward Batalha on 1 August 1983. The 36 route was unusual in that it left the outer terminus at Santo Ovidio towards the lower level of the bridge but then turns up the hill to join the 31 route also from Santo Ovidio. (D .R. Harvey)

Below: Driving over the decorative bricks in Praça da Batalha is trolleybus 47 in August 1988. This one-man-operated Dalfa-bodied Lancia 103 type has arrived from Santo Ovidio and carries a virtually complete complement of passengers of which only 29 were seated. It did have the capability of carrying another 47 standee passengers. The trolleybus is carrying on its side panel an advertisement for Whyte & Mackay's Scotch blended whisky, which was popular at that time in Portugal. (D. R. Harvey)

Above: Until the twenty-first century, many of the buildings had extra storeys added on to the original structure giving a very ramshackled appearance; the building with the washing hanging from the balconies just to the left of the trolleybus is one of these slum properties, which might look quaint but in reality they must have been frightful to live in, being a vertical version of a favela. Speeding up the steep hill from the São Bento Railway Station in Avenida de Dom Alfonso Henriques on 29 August 1986 is Dalfa-bodied Lancia single-decker 48 (98) working on the busy 33 route to Coimbões. Like all of these 25 trolleybuses, 48 was taken out of service in March 1993. (P. J. Thompson)

Opposite above: Lancia trolleybus 48 (98) with a Dalfa body passes the impressive entrance to the Estação São Bento as it crosses the Rua de Almeida Garrett in the mid-1980s. It is working on the 36 to Santo Ovidio on a bright summer's day. Unusually, one of the saloon's side windows has its sun blind fully pulled down while the one behind it has its blind half pulled down. The bus following the trolleybus is 520 (ON-17-77), a Volvo B58-55P dating from October 1973 and fitted with a Salvador Caetano B36D body. It was rebodied in June 1985 with a new CAMO body and remained in service until the 512–572 suffered a mass withdrawal in 1996 and 1998. (P. M. Photography)

Below: Turning right at the Art Deco-inspired Cinema Batalha in Praça da Batalha is Dalfa-bodied Lancia 103 type single-decker trolleybus 50 (100) returning from Santo Ovidio in August 1988. Behind the trolleybus is the 1866 statue of King Pedro V of Portugal. He was born on 16 September 1837 and became King of Portugal in 1853, being nicknamed 'the Hopeful'. Under his popular though tragically short reign, roads, education, telegraphs, and railways were constructed and improvements in public health were made. Unfortunately the health improvements did not help the longevity of either his German wife Queen Stephanie, who died in 1858 after less than one year of marriage from diphtheria, or the king, who succumbed to typhoid fever at the age of 24 on 11 November 1861. It was a great tragedy...hence the statue! (D. R. Harvey)

The last of the 25 Dalfa B29D bodied Lancia Type 103s was 51 (101). This was the bus chosen for the official photograph when new in 1967. These modern, rather handsome trolleybuses had a strikingly deep red livery on the lower panels, white window surrounds and a grey roof. It had two wide doors, the front one for entering the trolleybus and the rear one for leaving. They also had standing space for a further 47 passengers. (STCP)

101-50 Lancia double-deckers

Approaching Bolhao in the Oporto city centre in August 1984 when working on the 11 route from San Pedro Da Cova, the most easterly of the trolleybus routes, is 101 (27). This was the first of the 50 Lancia 103 chassis fitted with CGE 150 hp motors and regenerative braking. At 36 ft long, these two-axle double-deckers had stylish Dalfa H43/25D bodywork with commodious entrance doors behind the rear axle that were guarded by a seated conductor. The exit was in the overhang beyond the setback front axle. There were two staircases, the rear one for entering passengers and the front one, controlled by the driver for those leaving the trolleybus. The trolleybus is in its original dark red and white livery. (D. R. Harvey)

Above: Travelling out of Oporto in August 1984 is 102 (28). This Dalfa-bodied Lancia double-decker is operating on the 12 route to Gondomar and is passing through the linear suburban development near to São Caetano when carrying a full complement of passengers. It is by now painted in the orange and white livery. This trolleybus was preserved after being withdrawn along with the rest of the class in March 1995 and was restored in the Transport Museum in Oporto. (D. R. Harvey)

Below: In 1959, the 3 tram route to Lordelo, west of the city centre, was one of the first three to be converted to single-deck trolleybus operation as the 35 route. This allowed the new fleet of BUT LETB1s access to the trolleybus depot at Carcereira, which was the main works until the purpose-built Areosa depot was opened in 1968. This pioneering trolleybus route had its terminus in the Rua Do Campo Alegre in Lordelo. It then headed almost due east to Largo Do Viriato before crossing the Avenida da Liberdade, located behind the trolleybus, whereupon the route originally terminated in the adjacent Praça de Almeida Garrett, which Lancia double-decker trolleybus 103 (239) is approaching. On 4 March the 35 route was extended to Campanhã Railway Station in Bonfim as the 35A and it is on this route which 103 is being employed. (R. Symons)

Above: Lancia double-decker 105 (31) works on a short working to San Roque along the Rua De San Roque de Lameira. The upper deck of the Dalfa-bodied trolleybus, which had a capacity of 43 passengers, is nearly empty as it approaches the San Roque terminus in August 1984. 105 retains its original dark red and white livery, which by this time was being phased out by the somewhat insipid orange and white colours. (D. R. Harvey)

Opposite above: Waiting at the traffic lights in São Caetano is a Dalfa-bodied Lancia Type 103. 106 (32) is travelling eastwards away from Oporto when working on the 11 service to São Pedro da Cova in August 1985. The trolleybus is about to turn left towards Santa Eulalia, which is a section of its route that it shares with the 12 route to Gondomar. The trolleybus is carrying an advertisement for Aguardente Antiqua, a 38 per cent proof golden coloured digestive wine that has been aged for five years in Portuguese oak barrels. (D. R. Harvey Collection)

Below: The design of the Dalfa bodies on the Lancia double-deckers had their origins in the 82-111 class of Leyland Atlantean LPDR1/1s of 1962, later renumbered as 221–259. The Metro-Cammell H41/32F bodies were derived from bus 72 (CE-57-02) and delivered in May 1962. The main differences between the Dalfa trolleybus bodies built for the Lancia double-decker and the Atlanteans was that the underfloor mounted CGE 130 hp motor required that the floor level of the otherwise flat lower saloon was a step higher. This also allowed for the lower side ventilation slots to be mounted in the lower side body panels. Thus the trolleybuses were higher than the motorbuses. 106 (32) loads up at the turning circle at the terminus of the 12 route in the town of Gondomar, with its destination blind already turned back in readiness for its return to Bolhao. (D. R. Harvey Collection)

Above: Lancia double-decker 107 (33) is parked in Areosa depot yard alongside the perimeter fencing and at the front of a line of other similar trolleybuses on 14 August 1990. Some three years earlier the trolleybus fleet had been repainted into orange and white with 146 (72) being the last. Despite its apparent excellent condition, all of the 101–150 class of Dalfa-bodied double-deckers would be withdrawn in March 1995. After that, the Oporto system hiccoughed its way to a final closure on 27 December 1997, ostensibly because of major roadworks near to this depot, but in reality because of the lack of political will to operate trolleybuses anymore! (D. R. Harvey)

Opposite above: Using its regenerative equipment as it descends one of the many steep hills on its way back to the Bolhao terminus in Oporto from Gondomar on the 12 route is red and white painted 108 (34). Carrying a full load, this Dalfa-bodied trolleybus is near to São Caetano on the Rua De San Roque Do Lameira during August 1984. This road was a strange mixture of old farm buildings (such as that on the extreme left), factories, warehouses and quite luxurious 1970s houses, interspersed with plots of land devoted to viticulture. The road surface was at this time made up of stone setts which were by now very uneven, causing the double-decker trolley bus bodies to rattle quite alamingly. (D. R. Harvey)

Opposite below: A further line of three Lancia Type 103 double-deckers is parked around the perimeter of Areosa depot on 14 August 1990 with trolleybus 108 (34) again, but by now painted in the orange and white livery, at the back of the queue. The rear of the Dalfa body reveals the pair of trolley retrievers beneath the rear lower saloon windows. As with the upper saloon rear windows, neither opens as an emergency exit and in order to affect a quick exit, a small hammer was provided to smash the glass and so get out quickly. (D. R. Harvey)

Above: The trolleybus terminus for the three trolleybus services going to the east of Oporto was in Bolhao at the rear of the splendid meat, fish, fruit, flowers and vegetable market dating from 1914 in Rua Alexandre Braga. Leaving the terminus is Dalfa-bodied Lancia Type 103 double-decker 109 (35) bound for São Pedro Da Cova on the 11 route in August 1984. The trolleybus is in its original livery though the panel between the decks is painted orange as the background colour as an advertisement is yet to be fitted. (D. R. Harvey)

Opposite above: Seen from the top deck of another trolleybus is 110 (36), a double-decker Lancia with a Dalfa body. It is travelling back to Bolhao in August 1984 and is passing through the linear urbanised area near San Roque, which at that time was a mixture of three-storey apartments and single-storey, very run-down nineteenth century cottages. The trolleybus is passing a short row of shops with the inevitable bar as well as overtaking a Renault 5 car. (D. R. Harvey)

Opposite below: Travelling down the hill in Rua Alexandre Braga as it tries to leave Bolhao in August 1988 is a Lancia double-decker. It appears to be stuck in a traffic jam behind a single-decker motorbus. 111 (37) is working on the São Pedro Da Cova on the 11 route and is adorned above the windscreen with an advertisement for Euromalha, which was a type of fabric to make sweaters and jumpers. The young boy standing on the platform looks fascinated at the trolleybus driver's controls. (D. R. Harvey)

Above: 112 (38) has just turned from the Rua da Fernandas Tomás into Rua Alexandre Braga to travel down the hill to its Bolhao terminus on 17 August 1990. Two members of the STCP traffic department, a driver and a supervisor, look as though they have found the correct trolleybus allocated for the driver to continue his next turn of duty. Through the windscreen of the trolleybus is the ticket machine suggesting that this Dalfa-bodied Lancia 103 has by now been converted o-m-o. (D. R. Harvey)

Opposite above: Parked in Areosa depot yard is 113 (39). These Lancia trolleybuses had bodies built by Dalfa with a H43/25D+15 standees layout. They had a rear entrance that utilised the space where the Diesel engine would have been on the 1962 Dalfa-bodied Leyland Atlantean LPDR1/1s. There were six inset steps in the thick rear body pillar in front of the rear doors, which gave a brave electrical engineer either the option of clambering up on to the roof to affect a repair when necessary or to spectacularly fall off the steps and be badly injured! The trolleybus also had two staircases and a front exit opposite the driver's cab. (D. R. Harvey)

Opposite below: Double-decker trolleybus 114 (40) is carrying a full load when it was operating on the 11 route to São Pedro Da Cova. It has just left the city centre and is in the Rua De San Roque Do Lameira heading north eastwards during August 1984. The Lancia 103 trolleybus still has its Dalfa bodywork painted in the attractive original dark red and white livery with a light grey roof and is carrying an advertisement for Sanjo leisure and sports shoes and trainers. (D. R. Harvey)

Above: Trolleybus 115 (41) has just crossed the southern end of the Avenida da Liberdade and is passing into the adjacent Praça de Almeida Garrett, which the Lancia double-decker trolleybus is approaching. It is travelling on the 35 route to Campanhã Railway Station in Bonfim in 1972. Not only does the elegant building in the distant Avenida da Liberdade have a large advertisement for Porto Sandeman but so does the trolleybus. In the panel between the decks is the well-known logo that features the black silhouette of a man dressed in a Portuguese student's cape and a wide Spanish hat, which is displayed across the city of Oporto. (D. R. Harvey Collection)

Opposite above: Rows of UTIC-bodied BUT LETB1s single-deckers are parked in Areosa trolleybus depot on 14 August 1990. 117 (43), a Lancia type 103, passes between the BUTs on a trial spin around the large open depot yard after being cleaned in the automatic bus wash. This was an example of the extremely good practice of STCP whose fleet was almost immaculately presented. These Lancias had a very uncomfortable-looking driving position; they had an almost vertical steering column coupled to an almost horizontal steering wheel. Despite this, they were well-liked by their drivers. (D. R. Harvey)

Below: Approaching the Gondomar terminus when working on the 12 route is Lancia double-decker 118 (44). Passing a haulier's yard with three canvas tilt-bodied lorries, the area had been recently developed with modern houses and apartments replacing numerous local vineyards. In August 1984 the Dalfa-bodied trolleybus is still in its 1966 livery. 118 is travelling over the somewhat worn cobbled road surface and is passing the parked, somewhat utilitarian-designed Renault 5 car. (D. R. Harvey)

Above: Parked front-to-front are two of the Dalfa H43/25D bodied Lancia 103S. The nearside rear view of trolleybus 119 (45) reveals the long rear overhang behind the back axle. Just visible through the open rear doors is the former position of the conductors counter. By 14 August 1990, these two-door trolleybuses are being worked as o-m-o vehicles with the passenger flow being reversed and the driver collecting the fares; passengers now board at the front below the ENTRADA sign and alight at the rear were the sign reads SAIDA (exit), thus making the conductor's counter redundant and subsequently removed allowing for more standing passengers on the rear platform. The other identical trolleybus awaiting a repair is 128 (54) with its front panel removed. (D. R. Harvey)

Above: A two-door CAMO-bodied Volvo B10M-55, 852 (RN-59-71), loads up with passengers when working on the 20 route. A Lancia trolleybus 122 (48) turns left from Rua Alexandre Braga into Rua Formosa in Bolhao as it follows another double-decker travelling into the eastern suburbs. The trolleybus, now painted in the orange and white livery is actually not in service and is probably returning to its depot having completed its duties on the 12 route. As with all the double-deckers this trolleybus would be prematurely taken out of service in March 1995. (D. R. Harvey)

Opposite below: Passing through Santa Eulalia and heading off to the south east on the long straight road to Gondomar on the 12 service is Lancia trolleybus 120 (40). This almost village-like landscape is actually part of a long linear urban development to the east of Oporto that is traversed by the 10, 11 and 12 trolleybus routes. The urban infilling along the main road has all but swallowed up the outlying towns of San Roque, São Caetano, Venda Nova, Santa Eulalia, São Pedro Da Cova and Gondomar but has left the agricultural land immediately behind the houses largely unaltered. (D. R. Harvey)

Above: Lancia double-decker 123 (49) stands empty on the hill in Rua de Sá da Bandeira in August 1985 when being overtaken by a somewhat battered Citroen Dyane saloon fitted with an improved 602cc two-cylinder engine. This busy city centre street was on the western side of the famous Bolhao under-cover market and was used for trolleybuses waiting to get onto the services running out to the east of Oporto. Unusually, this orange and white liveried trolleybus carries no advertisements. (D. R. Harvey)

Opposite above: Standing at the San Pedro Di Cova terminus of the 11 route in August 1985 is 124 (50); a red and white-liveried Lancia Type 103 double-decker trolleybus. The neat-looking Dalfa two-door 68-seater bodywork is due for its first repaint as it is still in the original deep red livery with white window surrounds. San Pedro Di Cova was the most rural of the three eastern routes and had the final run in to the terminus along roads surrounded by fields of grape vines. (D. R. Harvey)

Below: The nearside view of Lancia Type 103 Dalfa double-decker trolleybus 124 (50) on the same day at the San Pedro da Cova terminus of the 11 route in August 1985, shows off the body's somewhat higher rear entrance platform steps. 124 is parked at the terminal loop still in the original deep red and white livery although all the between side panels have been besmirched with an advertisement for Palvopan kitchen equipment. This 1966-built trolleybus has lost its upper front window opening ventilators but still retains those swivelling lower opening windscreen windows. When the latter were removed, STCP received a large number of complaints from the by now sweaty drivers! (D. R. Harvey)

Above: A row of double-decker Lancia Type 103s are lined up in Rua da Alegria waiting to take their slot in the trolleybus extras required during the afternoon peak. Leading the three Dalfa-bodied trolleybuses is 124 (50), which on moving away, may well turn left and travel to Bonfim, although in all likelihood it will go onto the Rua Alexandre Braga termini in Bolhao. (P. M. Photography)

Above: The 12 route to Gondomar passed through some distinctly varied urban landscapes with run-down nineteenth century buildings and mid-twentieth century developments. Dalfa-bodied Lancia trolleybus 126 (52) has just descended the distant hill and is travelling away from the city centre on its way to Gondomar in August 1984. As per usual on this busy route, the double-decker is carrying a good number of passengers. One of the better conceived features of the Dalfa-bodies was the roof line and the smoothly designed front dome. (D. R. Harvey)

Opposite below: Being employed on the 11 route, Lancia Type 103 double-decker trolleybus 125 (51), is in Rua Calçada de Baixo. Carrying a very large advertisement for Kenwood kitchens, 125 is on its way to Sao Pedro da Cova on 18 February 1987 about half full with passengers. The thicker pillars at the front and rear of the saloon carry the electrical cables from the overhead electrical wiring to the underfloor mounted CGE 150 hp traction motors, although the rear was particularly useful in order to strengthen the bodywork. (D. R. Harvey Collection)

Above: Travelling along the Rua da Bonfim behind a Renault 5 saloon car is Dalfa-bodied Lancia 127 (53). Behind it is a British-built BMC JU 250 van. The trolleybus is about to fork to the right into Rua de Fernandes Tomás, which will take the trolleybus to the Bolhao city centre terminus in Rua Alexandre Braga. It is arriving on the 10 route from Venda Nova when still fairly new and still prone to look a little down at the front end. At their first overhaul their front suspension would be suitably adjusted. (P. M. Photography)

Opposite above: Parked in front of Caetano B32D-bodied Volvo B58-55F 673 (PO 74-87), dating from November 1977 in the Rua Alexandre Braga, is double-decker trolleybus 128 (54). This Lancia Type 103 had a seating capacity layout of 34/29 and is already fairly full with passengers who are preparing for the seven-mile journey to Gondomar having boarded the trolleybus via the back door and paid the seated conductor at his counter. (P. M. Photography)

Below: With the author's wife Diana sitting in the front seat of the offside of the upper deck, Lancia trolleybus 130 (56) stands alongside the small cigarette and confectionary kiosk located at the terminus. It was very hot day in August 1984 at the turning circle at Gondomar. 130 loads up before returning back to Bolhao in Oporto on the 12 route. Beyond the benches are two local independent coaches that serve the smaller outlying villages and work the school runs. (D. R. Harvey)

Above: Powering its way up the steep hill in the Rua 31 de Janeiro is Dalfa-bodied Lancia double-decker trolleybus 131 (57) on its way to the Praça da Batalha. It is being closely followed by one of the Daimler CVD6 single-deckers on 22 September 1972. At the bottom of the hill on the right between the trolleybus and the distant church and just in front of the nearest of the three four-wheeler trams is the entrance to the Praça de Liberdade. In the distance is the Baroque-styled Igreja dos Clérigos. The church was completed in 1750. The main façade of the church is heavily decorated with baroque motifs such as garlands and shells. The monumental bell tower of the church, inspired by Tuscan campaniles is located at the back of the building. It is an impressive 250 feet high and was built between 1754 and 1763. (C. C. Thornburn)

Opposite below: The Igreja de Santo Ildefonso is an eighteenth-century church constructed in granite and is located in the historic Praça da Batalha. It was initially opened in 1730, and was completed in 1739 by the addition of the two bell towers. The church was built in Baroque style and a twentieth-century façade was added consisting of about 11,000 distinctive azulejos tiles covering the front of the church, which was completed in November 1932. In July 1967, when only a few weeks old, Lancia double-decker trolleybus 132 (58) is being chased into the square by an Opel Kadett and a Peugeot 403 while working on the 36 route to Santo Ovidio. (R. Symons)

Opposite above: Lancia trolleybus 131 (57) works into Bolhao on the 11 route from San Pedro da Cova when still in its original red and white livery. It has just passed the O Nosso café in its 1950s apartment block and stands beneath the large letter S on the overhead wires signifying the position of the bus stop in a tree-lined open space at the edge of Oporto's central area. On the side of the Dalfa-bodied double-decker is an advertisement for Coute toothpaste, which was developed in 1930s and played an important role in changing oral hygiene habits in Portugal. (P. M. Photography)

Above: In August 1984, on its way to San Pedro Da Cova on the 11 route is a very well-laden Dalfa-bodied Lancia double-decker 134 (60). It is passing through the nineteenth and twentieth century-built linear suburban development near to São Caetano. 134 is in a long line of traffic on a very steep section of the Rua De São Roque De Lameira. In the distance at the back of the same traffic jam is another Lancia double-decker, which unlike 134, is in the later orange and white livery. Parked on the left is a German-made NSU Prinz 4, a small two-door, two-cylinder 598 cc rear engine saloon. (D. R. Harvey)

Opposite above: Parked alongside each other in the huge expanse of Areosa depot yard on Tuesday 14 August 1990 is the double-deck and single deck version of the Dalfa bodies mounted on the Lancia Type 103 chassis. On the left is 134 (60), one of the 50 double-deckers supplied to STCP in 1966, while next to it is single-decker 46 (96). The obvious similarities are their fronts, which have virtually the same front aprons and windscreen arrangements, whereas the lower saloon windows on 134 have vertical pillars, the front and rear bays on 46 have sloping saloon windows. The chassis' were virtually identical and while clearly 46 has no top deck it does share the same roof-mounted trolley shields as its larger cousin. (D. R. Harvey)

Below: Turning from the Rua da Fernandas Tomás into Rua Alexandre Braga is Lancia trolleybus 135 (61). The Dalfa bodies at first sight looked as though they were mounted on the slightly earlier Leyland Atlanteans delivered to Oporto a few years earlier. In fact they were two-doored vehicles, sat higher off the ground and had quite a long rear overhang when compared to the Leylands. 135 has returned from San Pedro Da Cova to Bolhao in August 1988. Located on this corner is a typical Portuguese decorative pavement made up of bands of different coloured setts that form an attractive mosaic pattern. (D. R. Harvey)

Above: One parked, one seemingly abandoned! In Areosa depot yard on 14 September 1990, 134 (64) has just been abandoned in the depot yard having just come off service. On the right in the shadow of one of the depot's covered maintenance bay's is the neatly parked 144 (70). Both of these Lancia Type 103 trolleybuses had Dalfa H43/25D bodywork and had entered service in the spring of 1966. In the early 1980s a start was made on repainting them from their original distinguished deep red and white livery into the corporate Portuguese livery of orange and white. In so doing they lost a little of the individuality of the Oporto trolleybus fleet. Shame! (D. R. Harvey)

Above: Travelling on the road out of Travagem on the 29 route to the Santa Caterina terminus in the Rua de Sa De Bandeira, in the Bolhao area of Oporto, is Dalfa-bodied Lancia double-decker 139 (65). It is passing stone walls behind which are vines on the right and cabbages on the left; a fairly typical use of the land in and around the Douro Valley. The trolleybus is still almost new as it is in its original deep red and white livery and still retains its opening front ventilators. Presumably it had been decided in the mid-1980s that the deep opening sliders in the deep saloon side windows would provide adequate ventilation, even in the hot Portuguese summers. (D. R. Harvey Collection)

Opposite below: Opened to Travagem in November 1968, the 29 route followed the line of the 9 service before being extended northwards. The 29 route shared the same city centre terminus as the more frequent 9 route in the Rua de Sa De Bandeira at the small Santa Caterina terminus. Standing behind the double-decker is 41 (91), a Dalfa-bodied Lancia single-decker, being used on the 9 service to Ermesinde. A certain amount of redevelopment work had taken place in the late 1960s but generally the late nineteenth-century buildings survived. (D. R. Harvey)

Above: Some of the most spectacular trolleybus routes in the world were those that crossed the River Douro on the upper level of Ponte de Luis I. What made them even more stunning was riding on the top deck of a double-decker. Lancia Type 103 140 (66) is travelling over the bridge from Vila Nova de Gaia towards the Avenida da Dom Afonso Henriques and down the hill to the Estação de São Bento. The trolleybus is still in its red and white livery and is working on an unnumbered short working to Camara de Gaia near to the Vila Nova de Gaia's Town Hall. Part of the skyline, the Mosteiro da Serra do Pilar, is prominently situated high above the River Douro and was completed in the late seventeenth century. (R. Symons)

Opposite above: STCP 140, a 1968 Lancia trolleybus with Dalfa H43/25D body, is negotiating the turning circle at Alto da Serra in Central Gondomar some half a mile from the Gondomar terminus. The turning circle was used for short workings back to Bolhao and 140 is waiting to return to the city centre on 14 August 1985. The trolleybus is being operated with a conductor and the front doors are being used as the exit. (D. R. Harvey Collection)

Opposite below: Oporto trolleybus 140 (66, again!) was brought to the UK for preservation by the Trolleybus Museum at Sandtoft. It arrived at the museum in 1996 and was used periodically until it suffered electrical problems and was placed into store. Before this happened, it was exhibited for the first time at the 1997 Sandtoft Gathering where it was parked on 27 July 1997 looking in really excellent condition. It is in the post mid-1980s orange, white and grey livery. Its passenger doors have been reversed in order that it can be used as a one-man-trolleybus. (D. R. Harvey)

Above: Leaving São Pedro da Cova trolleybus terminus, with the turning circle behind the trolleybus, is 141 (67). The Lancia double-decker is on its way back to Bolhao in Oporto early in its career with the Dalfa H43/25D in the dark red and white livery. The rural nature of the area around the terminus in this part of the Douro Valley is devoted to viticulture as well as the growing of vegetables. The grapes are grown for the magnificent Vinho Verde, a green-tinted, refreshingly light sparkling wine. (D. R. Harvey Collection)

Above: Dalfa H43/25D bodied Lancia trolleybus 143 (69) is approaching Oporto's city centre when working on the 12 route from Gondomar. It is a hot Portuguese summer's day as all of the sliding saloon ventilators are wide open and some of the lower saloon's window blinds have been pulled down. The orange and white-painted Lancia double-decker was modified in the mid-1980s when the windscreen opening windows and the upper saloon front window hoppers were removed. They would have been more than welcome on this sweltering day. (D. R. Harvey)

Opposite below: Parked in Areosa trolleybus depot on 14 August 1990 are 142 (68) and 125 (51). These Lancia Type 103 Dalfa–bodied double-deckers had been by now been painted in the orange and white livery. From this angle the rear staircase is visible in front of the thicker rear body pillar while the second staircase, both built somewhat unusually without vertical step risers, was located immediately at the back of the covered panel behind the drivers cab. These 50 double-deckers were bought for use mainly on the long and heavily subscribed 11, 12 and 13 services to the east of the city. They were also used on the 29 service to Travagem as well as the 31 and 36 services to Santo Avidio and the 33 route to Coimbões, all of which used the top level of the Ponte de Dom Luis I. (D. R. Harvey)

Above: A very steamed up 144 (70) is being used on the 35 route to Campanhã to the east of the city near to the Estação Campanhã. Standing on the cobbles on 24 March 1973, in the original dark red and white livery, the trolleybus still has its opening ventilator at the bottom of the windscreen and in the front upper saloon. Behind the trolleybus is a row of typical nineteenth century buildings with Juliette balconies with small iron railings. (F. Hornby)

Opposite above: Grumbling over the stone setts at the terminal loop at the 12 terminus at Gondomar in 1971 is Lancia double-decker trolleybus 144 (70) in almost original condition, although the upper saloon opening front ventilators have been replaced by fixed glass. The down-at-heel buildings at the end of the line at Gondomar that stand behind the trolleybus, contrast with the appearance of the smartly presented Dalfa bodywork on the Lancia Type 103 chassis. (D. R. Harvey Collection)

Below: Most of the urban roads throughout Portugal were constructed of durable stone blocks and on the trolleybus routes in Oporto. Having been driven at great speed over the indifferent road surfaces, the bodies of these poor trolleybuses (despite being well constructed) rattled, creaked and groaned disconcertingly with their suspension thumping over the uneven road surface. Lancia trolleybus 145 (71) works over this type of poor road service on the 12 route from Gondomar to Bolhao in August 1984, passing an old cottage daubed with graffiti encouraging people to vote for the Communist Party. (D. R. Harvey)

Above: Near to the terminus of the 11 route at São Pedro da Cova, 146 (72) prepares to return to the city centre at Bolhao. The driver is turning the destination blind and is being watched by the young girl to the left of the trolleybus. The grey-painted front dome of the Dalfa body shows some signs of tree damage, but the rest of the vehicle looks in fine fettle. It carries a large side panel advertisement for Móveis Fetex, a quality furniture manufacturer based in Gondomar. (D. R. Harvey Collection)

Below: Loading up in the Rua Alexandre Braga just before 7 pm on 26 August 1986 are two of the Lancia double-decker trolleybuses bodied with Dalfa H43/25D+15 standee passengers. The nearest trolleybus, going to São Pedro da Cova on the 11 route is 147 (73). Behind it is 142 (68) working on the 12 route to Gondomar. Even in the early evening, the trolleybuses are getting remarkably full. Noticeable is that both trolleybuses are still operating with conductors as their front doors are firmly shut and the passengers are loading at the rear. The conversion of the trolleybuses to o-m-o began in 1967. Unlike 142, the leading trolleybus still retains its lower opening front windscreen. (P. J. Thompson)

Above: Having just arrived at the top end of the Rua Alexandre Braga and unloaded their passengers, the driver and conductor of 149 (75) stand at the front doors of their Dalfa-bodied Lancia trolleybus for a brief natter, before trundling down the hill to their trolleybus stop on 22 August 1987. They have been working the 10 route from the largely residential suburb of Venda Nova, which was the shortest of the three eastern routes operated by double-deckers in Oporto. (P. J. Thompson)

Below: Parked over the maintenance pits in the vehicle repair bay at the Areosa trolleybus depot is Lancia 150 (76), the last of the 50 Dalfa-bodied double-deckers. On 14 August 1990, it has its front panel removed prior to some remedial work. In front of the slightly curious mechanic are two racks of springs bearing testament to the previously mentioned poor road surfaces in the city over which the trolleybuses had to run. On the left are two unidentified double-deckers, with the leading one seemingly with quite a few damaged lower side panels. (D. R. Harvey)

The short wheelbase 1985-vintage single-deckers

Above: Passing the Infante tram terminus of route 1 is EFA/CEG 175TR trolleybus 61 (152). The vehicle has a Caetano B32D body. It is working on the 49 route introduced in 1992 from Hospital São João to Alfandega and the former Customs House built in the Neoclassical style in 1822 just a few hundred yards away on the banks of the River Douro. The Porto Customs House is now a state-of-the-art convention centre. Towering above the trolleybus is the seventeenth-century São Francisco Church, which looks largely Gothic-styled from the outside, but is flamboyantly decorated internally in a heavily gilded Baroque style. (D. R. Harvey)

Opposite above: Picking up passengers in front of the wonderful Café do Brasileira in August 1985 is EFA/CEG 175TR 62 (153) with a Caetano B32D body. It is on the 36 route to Santo Ovidio, which crosses the River Douro by way of the upper level of the Ponte de Dom Luis I. These trolleybuses had a 175 hp Éfácéc electric motor with some components manufactured by Kiepe. In addition the fifteen trolleybuses were equipped with a 67 hp Hatz diesel engine allowing them to manoeuvre away from the overhead. Unfortunately, the powerful electric motors on these comparatively small trolleybuses consumed far more electricity than the earlier trolleybuses and to some extent this began to eek into the financial stability of the STCP. After the end of double-decker operation in March 1995, there seemed little justifiable reason to keep the remnant of the once 126 vehicle strong system in operation and it was subsequently closed down on 27 December 1997. (D. R. Harvey)

Below: The boxy-looking Caetano B32D bodied 63 (154) is standing in front of the Art deco-styled Cinema Batalha in August 1985. This EFA/CEG175TR single-decker is shortly going to leave its terminus in Batalha on the 33 service to Coimbroes, although it is nearly empty. Introduced in 1983, the 61–75 batch of trolleybuses were, with their auxiliary Hatz diesel engines, 'state-of-the-art' as far as small single-decker trolleybuses were concerned. With a 175 hp rated electric motor they were almost too powerful and certainly used far too much electricity. As a result of civil engineering works in central Oporto and a lack of political direction by the city council, the system was prematurely closed leaving these fourteen-year-old trolleybuses without anywhere to run. Of the fifteen vehicles comprising the 61–75 numbered trolleybuses, all but trolleybus 74, which was sold to Coimbra, were bought by the Almaty system in Kazakhstan in 2000 and were repainted in the white and pale yellow livery of that city. (D. R. Harvey)

Above: Passing Sao Bento Railway Station in Praça Almeida Garrett is Caetano-bodied EFA/ CEG175TR 63 (154). It is working on the 33 route to Coimbroes and by way of contrast, when seen in Batalha, this single-decker is loaded to the gunwales with a near capacity of standing passengers. Behind the trolleybus is the Rua de Sá da Bandeira dominated at the junction with Almeida Garrett by the Church of Santo António dos Congregados. This church dates from the end of the seventeenth century and has a baroque facade covered by azulejos tiles. (D. R. Harvey)

Above: Looking down into the Praça de Batalha from the Hotel Império is trolleybus 65 (156), working on the 33 route to the south of the River Douro. This is an EFA/CEG 175TR trolleybus with a Caetano B32D body dated from March 1983 and actually suited the orange and white livery far more than the earlier trolleybuses. Behind the trolleybus in this impressive square with its geometrically laid out mosaic pavement is the 1866 statue of King Pedro V of Portugal (1837-1861), who was king of Portugal from 1853 but died at the prematurely young age of 24 having contracted typhoid fever. (D. R. Harvey)

Opposite below: 64 (155), a Caetano bodied EFA/CEG175TR, stands at the bus stop in front of the A Brasileira café in the Rua Sa de Bandeira in August 1985 when working on the 33 route to Coimbroes, not yet two years old. At the rear of these trolleybuses were the trolley retrievers whose ropes up to the trolley booms kept the heads taut and attached to the overhead wiring and in the event of a de-wirement prevented the trolley arms from flailing about. (D. R. Harvey)

Above: Turning into Rua Sá de Bandeira in the City Centre of Oporto in August 1988 is Caetano-bodied EFA/CEG175TR 66 (157). Working on the Coimbroes service, the trolleybus carries an advertisement almost for itself as the Efacec electrical company also supplied the electrical equipment for the trolleybus. The saloon section of the bus had a very disappointing, almost being a van-with-windows style which was a total mismatch with the almost standard Caetano bus front section. (D. R. Harvey)

Opposite above: Parked on Areosa depot yard on 14 August 1990 are four of the 61–75 class of EFA/CEG175TRs with the 31-seater Caetano bodies. From left to right is 67(158), 71 (162), 64 (155) and 73 (164). The orange and white livery rather suited these modern vehicles that were built in March 1983, but which had only another seven years of service left before being withdrawn. Despite being o-m-o modern single-deckers, they had four steps up into the saloon making them far from low-step entrance vehicles. (D .R. Harvey)

Below: Stuck in a traffic jam in August 1984 at the top of the hill in Avenida Dom Alfonso Henriques where it meets the Rua Saraiva Carvalho is 68 (159), one of the two door 31-seaters delivered in 1983. It is going to Santo Ovidio by way of the lower level of the Ponte de Do Luis I over the River Douro and then along the quayside below the port caves in Vila Nova de Gaia. Waiting alongside the trolleybus is a BMC Mini Mk II. (D. R. Harvey)

Above: Travelling into the City Centre in August 1984, 70 (161) speeds towards Rua Sá de Bandeira on the 32 route. This EFA/CEG175TR has a Caetano B31D body and was designed for o-m-o. The dual door layout was different from earlier single-deckers in that the second door was centrally mounted but both doors involved something of a clamber into the high-floored saloon. Somehow, although no doubt very efficient, the design of the body looked rather basic. (D. R. Harvey)

Above: About to pass underneath the Oporto portal at the end of the lower deck of the Ponte de Do Luis I is trolleybus 74 (165). The bridge, built by the Belgian firm of Willebroek, was opened in 1886 and was a two-level bridge. It echoes the Maria Pia railway bridge of 1877, designed by Gustav Eiffel, just upstream. This EFA/CEG175TR chassis and Caetano-bodied single-decker was the only one of the 61–75 class to escape being exported after the Oporto system closed to the Almaty system in Kazakhstan in 2000. 74 was sold to Coimbra becoming their fleet number 71 when it entered service there in September 2003. (D. R. Harvey)

Opposite below: The 61–75 class of 1983-built Caetano bodied EFA/CEG175TR single-deckers were usually used on the four routes across the River Douro by way of the Ponte de Do Luis I. 73 (164), is approaching Praça da Batalha when working on the 36 route. In August 1984, it is passing a shopping and office block designed in the 1920s with Art Deco windows, semi-circular windows and balconies. (D. R. Harvey)

The articulated last trolleybuses

Above: The last trolleybus bought by STCP were ten articulated single-deckers numbered 160–169, which entered service in 1985. The first one, 160 (186), stands partially inside the main maintenance facility at Areosa depot on 14 August 1990. With the warning notice VEICULO LONGO, which really does not require any translation, these Caetano/Efacec 175TR110s had Caetano AB41T bodies. Alongside the grill at the back of the bus was a Hatz diesel engine that allowed the bus to travel along roads where there was either no overhead or where it was being repaired. (D. R. Harvey)

Opposite above: The two-door front section of the Caetano articulated trolleybuses was very similar to the 61–75 class and although the seating split is unknown, the front half contained around 30 seats, many in forward facing rows, as did the rear section, where there were at least two rows of seats facing forward, as well as a bench seat opposite the rear doors. This gave a capacity of 41 seated passengers. Caetano/Efacec 175TR110s trolleybus 161 (187), is parked in Areosa depot yard on 14 August 1990. (D. R. Harvey)

Below: A rare view of Carcereira depot yard reveals that the only identifiable trolleybus in the yard available for service is 161 (187). Behind it are a number of withdrawn Lancia double-deckers and one of the 27–51 class of Lancia single-deckers. The date is sometime between March 1995, when the Lancias were all withdrawn, and December 1997 when the remnants of the Porto trolleybus system were withdrawn. Nine of the ten articulated 41-seater Caetano/Efacec 175TR110s were bought by the Almaty system in Kazakhstan in 2000, having been stored for three years but available to be demonstrated on a small section of overhead from the depot for the benefit of prospective customers. (Luisfer)

Above: Travelling down the steep hill in the Rua de Sa da Bandeira when working on the 29 route from Travagem is 162 (188), one of the Caetano/Efacec 175TR110s with Caetano AB41T bodywork. The trolleybus carries a number of advertisements for the AEG Lavamat washing machines. From the nearside rear, the front and rear sections of the articulated trolleybus body sections seem to be an unhappy marriage as they are set rather like a Dromedary camel's single hump with the concertina joint being at the top! All the electrical overhead was on the roof of the rear section of the articulated trolleybus and had access steps set into the bodywork on either side of the articulated centre section, though these were only fitted to the nearside of the vehicles. (P. J. Thompson)

Above: Turning into the Rua de Sa da Bandeira on 22 August 1987 is articulated Caetano/Efacec 175TR110 trolleybus 165 (191). Fitted with a Caetano AB41T body, it has briefly been in the shadows of the lush trees at the junction with the Rua de Gonçalo Cristóvão as it travels on an inbound journey from Travagem. Just visible through the trees on the other side of the small square is a Dalfa-bodied Lancia double-decker. (P. J. Thompson)

Opposite below: Friday 17 August 1990 was an extremely hot day and so the leisurely filling of the trolleybus was perhaps not too surprising. Gradually loading up with passengers at the 9 terminus at the small square at Santa Catarina near to Bolhao, is 163 (189). The articulated Caetano/Efacec 175TR110 was built in 1985 and is parked in front of one of the earlier Lancia single-deckers. Once loaded, 163 will begin its next tour of duty on the route to Ermesinde. (D. R. Harvey)

Above: 166 (192), accelerates down the hill in the Rua de Sa da Bandeira on 22 August 1987. The trolleybus is returning to Bolhao after working on the 29 service from Travagem. These articulated Caetano/Efacec 175TR110s were very powerful trolleybuses with Efacec electric motors of 280 hp but used far too much electrical current, which made them uneconomic to operate. Sister trolleybus 167 was intended to be preserved for the Oporto Museum but instead it was sold in 2003 to Coimbra as their fleet number 70; it was withdrawn by 2009. The others went in October 2000 to Almaty in Kazakhstan. (P. J. Thompson)

Below: 169 (195) was parked out of service in Areosa trolleybus depot yard on 14 August 1990. It does look a little unloved with a sign in the windscreen, suggesting that it has a fairly major electrical problem. With the amount of dust covering the bus it appears to have been out of service for some time. It would however go back into service and after three years of being left after its final withdrawal in December 1997. It was sold to Almaty in Kazakhstan in 2000 for further service. (D. R. Harvey)